Financial Literacy Basics:

Renting an Apartment & Understanding Renters' Insurance

Financial Literacy Basics:

Renting an Apartment & Understanding Renters' Insurance

2019/20 Edition

GREY HOUSE PUBLISHING

FINANCIAL RATINGS SERIES
WeissRatings
& Grey House Publishing

https://greyhouse.weissratings.com

Grey House Publishing
4919 Route 22, PO Box 56
Amenia, NY 12501-0056
(800) 562-2139

Weiss Ratings
4400 Northcorp Parkway
Palm Beach Gardens, FL 33410
(561) 627-3300

WeissRatings
Independent. Unbiased. Accurate. Trusted.

Published by Grey House Publishing, Inc., located at 4919 Route 22, Amenia, NY 12501; telephone 518-789-8700. Grey House Publishing neither guarantees the accuracy of the data contained herein nor assumes any responsibility for errors, omissions or discrepancies. Grey House Publishing accepts no payment for listing; inclusion in the publication of any organization, agency, institution, publication, service or individual does not imply endorsement of the publisher.

Grey House
Publishing

20189/20 Edition
ISBN: 978-1-64265-269-7

Table of Contents

Part 1: Renting an Apartment

Part 2: Understanding Renters' Insurance

Welcome!

Grey House Publishing and Weiss Ratings are proud to announce the third edition of *Financial Literacy Basics*. Each volume in this series provides readers with easy-to-understand guidance on how to manage their finances. Designed for those who are just starting out and for those who may need help handling their finances, volumes in this series outline, step-by-step, how to make the most of your money, which pitfalls to avoid, and what to watch out for, and give you the necessary tools to make sure you are fully equipped to manage your finances.

Volumes in this series take the guesswork out of financial planning—how to manage a checking account, how to stick to a budget, how to pay back student loans quickly—information necessary to get started on your financial future. Each volume is devoted to a specific topic. Combined, they provide you with a full range of helpful information on how to best manage your money. Individual volumes are:

- How to **Make and Stick to a Budget**
- How to **Manage Debt**
- Starting a **401(k)**
- Understanding **Health Insurance** Plans
- **Renting an Apartment** & Understanding **Renters Insurance**
- Understanding the **Cost of College, Student Loans** & How to Pay Them Back
- **Buying a Car** & Understanding **Auto Insurance**
- What to Know About **Checking Accounts**

Filled with valuable information alongside helpful worksheets and planners, these volumes are designed to point you in the right direction toward a solid financial future, and give you helpful guidance along the way.

Financial Literacy Basics:
Part 1: Renting an Apartment

Getting Ready to Rent an Apartment

Moving in to your first apartment can be a little frightening. You might be asking yourself: Can I afford the monthly rent? Will my landlord be fair? Are there other expenses that I should budget for? There are a lot of things to consider before you sign a lease to rent an apartment, to make sure that you are making the right decision for you, and for your budget.

Make a Budget for Rent

First, you want to make sure that you can afford your monthly rent. Write down how much you earn each month (income) and all of your monthly expenses. A good rule of thumb is that your rent should be no more than one third of your income. Make sure you allow for additional expenses you will have, as a renter, like groceries and utilities.

You can use the budget worksheets in another guide in this series, *Financial Literacy: How to Make & Stick to a Budget*, to help you get started.

Budget for Furnishings Too

You should budget for some basic furnishings as well, since you probably don't want to sleep on the floor. You'll need a bed, a couch, a table, chairs, cookware and utensils. Better yet, make sure your friends and family know that you are apartment shopping. They might be willing to donate second-hand furniture to your new apartment, or provide much-needed items as a gift or as a donation. Consignment stores, thrift shops, for sale sites and garage sales are all good ways to furnish a new apartment on a budget.

Searching for an Apartment

Take your time to shop around for an apartment. Make sure the location is convenient and safe. Is it close to your workplace? Is it close to shops, the grocery store, and restaurants? Are any of these places within walking distance? Is the neighborhood safe? Is a parking space available for you? Are there other tenants in the building? You're most likely going to live in your apartment for at least six months or a year, so it's important to make sure that you will be safe and comfortable in your space. If you are unsure about an apartment, keep shopping around until you find the right place.

Paperwork You'll Need

Before you start apartment shopping, you'll want to pull together some paperwork about yourself, since most landlords will require documentation as part of your application process. These items might include:

- Your driver's license

- Recent paystubs

- Resume

- Character references, from a boss, co-worker or professor

- Other official document, like registration for your car

What is a Lease?

A lease is a legal document between a property owner, most likely a landlord, and the tenant, the person who wants to occupy the property. The lease outlines all of the terms and conditions of the rental. It is a legal document. Once you sign it, you are bound by its terms, so make sure that you read everything and that you fully understand its meaning before you sign.

The following pages highlight some topics that you should discuss with a potential landlord when you're looking for an apartment, and make sure you understand before you sign your lease.

Upfront Costs

Most landlords require some payment upfront, before you can rent an apartment, so you might need to save up for a few months before you can start apartment shopping. It's typical to have to pay your first and last month's rent upfront. You might have to pay an additional security deposit, and application fees, too.

The Length of the Lease

Most people sign a one-year lease, but you do have other options. Some landlords will agree to a six-month or a month-to-month lease. If you're not sure about a particular neighborhood, you might want to ask for a six-month lease. If you might be moving in the near future, a month-to-month lease might work for you. Keep in mind that leases for shorter terms, like month-to-month, can be more expensive than a yearly lease. On the flip side, you might be able to get a discounted rate if you agree to a longer lease, like 18 months or two years. Make sure that you are willing to stay that long before you sign, since you might be penalized for terminating the lease early.

Security Deposit

A security deposit is a sum of money that you give your landlord to hold, to ensure that you meet your lease requirements. If damage is done to the apartment while you are a tenant, your landlord might deduct the repair costs from your security deposit. Some landlords require you to pay your last month's rent upfront, which acts as a security deposit of sorts too. Not all security deposits are refundable, so you'll want to read your lease carefully to be sure. If your security deposit is refundable, you may earn interest for the amount of time that your landlord held your security deposit.

Ongoing Costs

When you are shopping for an apartment, ask your prospective landlord if any utilities are included with your rent. If not, ask about how much your utilities will cost each month.

Specifically, find out about the costs for:

- Heat

- Gas

- Electricity

- Internet

- Water

- Trash Collection

- Lawn Service

- Snow Removal

What About a Roommate?

Before you sign a lease, see if your lease will allow a roommate. Some leases do and some do not, so read the lease carefully. You might not be renting with a roommate at first, but might want to add a roommate later. Make sure that the lease will allow you to add a roommate.

Consider carefully what living with a roommate would entail before going this route. Are you compatible? Is one person neat and the other messy? Does one person stay out late and the other gets up early for work? Will you both be able to afford your share of the rent? Making sure that you're going to enjoy sharing a living space, before you move in together, can save a lot of hassles and headaches down the road.

Make Sure All Roommates Sign the Lease!

If you are renting with a roommate, make sure that each roommate signs the lease, so that you are all covered under the agreement. That will protect you if your roommate just stops paying their share of the rent.

Pets

Not all landlords allow pets on their property, so it's important to ask before you sign a lease. Some rentals even have restrictions about the size of a pet, or about certain breeds. If you can bring your pet, you might have to pay an extra security deposit or additional fees.

Insurance

Does your landlord require renters' insurance? Some do, and some do not, so make sure you ask. Even if it's not required, you should still consider getting renters' insurance. Most renters' policies are not very expensive. The average cost is $17 per month, and if your property is damaged or stolen, you would be protected. You can find out more about renters' insurance in Part 2 of this guide.

Make sure that specifics about renewal and termination are included in your lease.

Policies & Rules

Ask your landlord about any policies that apply to the apartment. Are there quiet hours? What about overnight visitors? Some additional rules might discuss smoking, maximum occupancy, parking, storage, and landlord right of entry. You could be fined for not following the rules, so make sure you are aware of any policies before you rent.

Sublease Agreements

If you have to move out early, you may be able to sublet your apartment, which means that you find someone else to take over the rental until your lease is up. Some landlords require you to find a sublease tenant, but some landlords want to find a sublease tenant on their own. Make sure that the terms of the sublease are clearly identified in your lease.

Moving Out

Be sure to find out what is required when you move out. Do you have to give your landlord certain notice? What happens if you have to move out before that? If you terminate your lease early, will you have to pay a fine, or lose your security deposit? Sometimes you can't terminate your lease early, and have to pay your monthly rent until your lease is up.

Automatic Lease Renewal

Some leases are set up to renew automatically at the end of the lease. Other leases require that the tenant notify the landlord at a specific time whether or not they want to renew their lease, or if they plan to move out. In either case, make sure that you are aware of the policy and send notifications as required. If you don't notify your landlord that you plan to move within the right time frame, you could incur fines or lose your security deposit, so it's important to pay attention to these details.

Who is in Charge of Repairs & Maintenance?

You'll want to find out who is responsible for general repairs and maintenance. In most cases, the landlord is responsible for repairs and maintenance, but that's not always the case. Ask about repairs to major appliances, plumbing, doors and windows, exterior maintenance, etc. Making sure it is clear who pays for and performs routine maintenance, including lawn mowing and snow removal, and repairs up front will save you headaches down the road.

Beware of Verbal Promises

If your prospective landlord makes verbal promises that are not written down in the lease, then you are not protected. Make sure that everything you have

discussed is written down in the lease before you sign it.

Apartment Inspection

Before you sign a lease, inspect the apartment carefully. Look for dents or scratches in the walls, damage to floors, appliances, and windows. Note anything that was damaged before you rented the apartment, and take pictures. Have the landlord make note of the prior damage in writing, so you will not be responsible for those repairs later.

Read Your Lease Carefully

Read through your lease carefully. Make sure that you understand all of the items. If you have a question, ask for clarification. Make sure that everything you have discussed is written down in the lease.

Make sure your lease discusses the following:

- The property's address, the landlord's name and contact information

- Upfront fees, security deposits, monthly rental costs

- When your rent is due, where to send payment, acceptable forms of payment

- Any grace periods for late payments, or late fees

- Whether or not any utilities are included in your rent

- Who is responsible for maintenance and repair

- Pets

- Roommates

- Rules & Policies

- Notifications About Moving Out

- Early Termination Rules & Penalties

- Lease Renewal Terms

Signing a Lease

When you sign a lease, you are signing a legal contract and agreeing to all of the items discussed in your lease. Read

and understand everything in your lease before you sign it.

Keep a Copy of Your Signed Lease

Make sure you keep a copy of your lease. Many landlords will provide two copies for signature, so you each get to keep a copy. Store it in a safe place, so you can refer back to what you signed if any issues arise in the future.

Defaulting on a Lease

A lease is a legal contract, so in most cases it cannot be terminated or changed unless both the landlord and the tenant agree. If you default on your lease, and move out before your lease is up, you may have to pay each month's rent until your lease is up, and you might have to pay other fees and penalties, as spelled out in your lease agreement.

If you absolutely must leave your apartment before your lease is up, contact your landlord and give them as much advance notice as possible. Make sure your apartment is clean and free of damage. Your landlord might forgive some fees or penalties if you give them ample notice, but they are not required to do so. You can also try to negotiate with your landlord to come up with a compromise based on your unique situation. If you and your landlord agree to special terms, make sure to get those terms in writing.

If you move out of your apartment without your landlord's approval, you will be responsible for paying rent until the end of your lease. Your landlord could sue you for uncollected rent.

Exceptions for Victims of Domestic Violence

If you have a court order of protection and your safety is jeopardized by remaining in the apartment, you may be able to break the lease with ten days' notice to your landlord. If your landlord does not voluntarily release you from the lease after you provide proper written notice, you can ask the Family Court judge to order the lease terminated.

Exceptions for Military Personnel

If you are going into active military service, you can break the lease if it's in your name. You must notify the landlord in writing and provide a full month's notice.

Things Landlords Cannot Do

Even though the landlord owns the property, in most cases they cannot barge in without your approval. In most states, landlords have to give at least 24 hours' notice before they can enter your apartment, even for repairs or maintenance. In the event of an emergency, or if the landlord believes the property has been abandoned, these rules don't apply. These rules should be spelled out in your lease agreement.

Landlords cannot lock a tenant out of a property, or turn off their utilities. Landlords must follow the applicable laws in their state regarding eviction.

In most cases, landlords cannot increase rates or charge extra fees, unless those rate increases or fees are discussed in your lease agreement.

Landlords cannot discriminate, it's the law. Landlords cannot refuse an applicant based on race, color, national origin, sex, familial status or handicap.

Financial Literacy Basics:
Part 2: Understanding Renters' Insurance

Why Do You Need Renters' Insurance?

Most renters don't have renters' insurance. They think their landlord's insurance policy will pay for their personal property if their apartment is damaged or destroyed. This isn't true! If you rent, you need renters' insurance. Your landlord's insurance policy covers the cost to rebuild your apartment or the entire building, but it won't pay for your personal property.

Some renters don't bother with renters' insurance because they don't think they own anything valuable. Think for a moment about how much it would cost to replace the furniture in your apartment. What about your clothes? Your electronics? Add to these obvious items the cost of replacing everything else in your apartment—dishes, utensils, pots and pans, sheets, towels, etc. and you'll see that it would cost a great deal of money to replace your personal property.

Cost & Coverage

You might not think you can afford renters' insurance, but it is surprisingly inexpensive. It costs less than $20 per month. And, in addition to property loss, renters' insurance gives you liability coverage.

Liability insurance pays for the bodily injury and property damage of others who are in your apartment. Suppose you hire a painter and he trips over a loose floorboard in your apartment, falls, and hurts his back. Later, you get a letter from an attorney saying the painter is suing you. You did not mention the loose floorboard to the painter and were, therefore, negligent (or responsible) for the accident, and have to appear in court. Liability insurance protects you from having to pay fines from lawsuits like this.

Renters' insurance policies can even cover additional living expenses that you would incur if your apartment was damaged or destroyed. This type of insurance is also called loss of use. For example, if a fire destroys your apartment, you will have to live somewhere else until you find a new place or your apartment is repaired.

Renters' insurance can cover the cost of hotel bills and other expenses such as meals at restaurants while you are displaced. The maximum amount of this coverage and the length of time it lasts depend on the specific policy.

Types of Coverage

When you purchase renters' insurance, you can opt for one of two types of coverage:

- **Replacement Cost Coverage, also called Replacement Cost Value (RCV)**

  Replacement cost coverage pays for the cost to replace your items with new, similar items. It does not take into account depreciation or the condition of the property.

- **Actual Cash Value (ACV)**

  With actual cash value (ACV) coverage, your insurance pays you what your property was worth when it was destroyed. It takes into account usage and depreciation.

For example, suppose you had an older sofa in your apartment when the apartment was destroyed by a fire. You paid $500 for the new sofa many years ago. At the time of the fire, however, it was old and in rough shape, worth only about $100. With RCV coverage, your insurance company will pay you the amount of money needed to buy a new sofa that is similar to the $500 sofa you had in your apartment. With ACV coverage, you'd get $100 for your sofa. Replacement cost coverage is more expensive than ACV coverage but it might be the better option for you.

Deductible

Be aware that your renters' insurance policy will have a deductible. This is the amount of money you need to pay before the policy kicks in. You usually have the option to choose your deductible, for example, a $250 deductible or a $500 deductible. If you choose a $250 deductible, you pay for any loss that's $250 or less.

Suppose someone steals your bicycle, which was outside your apartment door. Your bike was worth about $150 and a new bike costs about $200. In this case, you could not file a claim for this loss because the cost to replace the bike is less than your $250 deductible. However, if there was a fire in your apartment and you lost $10,000 of personal property, you would pay the first $250 and your insurance company would pay for the rest.

In general, the higher a policy's deductible is, the lower the cost of the policy. Raising a deductible to $1,000 can decrease the cost of a policy by as much as 25 percent. Some companies offer a $0 deductible, which means you don't have to pay out of pocket for a claim; however, the cost of such a policy is higher than usual.

Renters' Insurance Covers Many Perils

Fire

Windstorm or Hail

Explosions

Theft

Covered Perils

Renters' insurance covers damage caused by a peril.

A peril is something that causes harm. Most renters' insurance policies are "named peril policies." If a peril isn't listed on the policy, you aren't covered for it.

The HO-4 is the most common renters' insurance policy. It offers protection against the following perils. See the Appendix for an explanation of each.

- Fire or lightning

- Windstorm or hail

- Explosion

- Riot or civil commotion

- Aircraft

- Vehicles

- Smoke

- Vandalism or malicious mischief

- Theft

- Volcanic eruption

- Falling objects

- Weight of ice, snow, or sleet

- Accidental discharge or overflow of water or steam

- Sudden and accidental tearing apart, cracking, burning, or bulging

- Freezing

- Sudden and accidental damage from artificially generated electrical current

Perils Not Covered

Renters' insurance policies do not cover property loss from floods and earthquakes. If you live in an area prone to floods or earthquakes, you need to purchase additional coverage to protect you against these perils.

- Flood

- Earthquake

Personal Property Covered

Personal property covered by a renters' insurance policy includes clothes, furniture, appliances, dishes, linens, and anything else you had in the apartment, including groceries and cleaning supplies.

Renters' insurance even covers personal property that is not on the premises. For example, it will cover the cost to replace your bike if it is stolen while you are at a park. It will cover personal property that was in your car if your car is destroyed.

However, some expensive personal items may have a cap on them. This is the maximum amount an insurance company will pay for the item. Electronics, such as televisions and computers, usually have a cap as do fine jewelry, furs, and firearms.

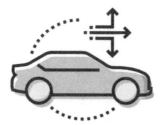

Personal Property Not Covered

Most renters' insurance policies have exclusions. Personal property that is excluded is not covered by a renters' insurance policy. Most policies exclude animals, birds, and fish. They also exclude automobiles and the personal property of guests at your apartment. In addition, renters' insurance usually does not cover loss or damage due to the following:

- Water backup through sewers and sump pumps

- A power outage

- Any type of war

- Governmental action, such as the seizure of property

- Sinkholes

Additional Coverage

You can purchase additional coverage for items capped or excluded in your renters' insurance policy by adding endorsements and floaters.

Endorsements

Also called trailers or riders, endorsements provide additional coverage for specific categories of items, such as jewelry and firearms.

For example, let's say you purchase a renters' insurance policy that covers up to $20,000 of personal property, with a cap of 10% of this amount (or $2,000) for electronics equipment. If your television, computer, and video-game system are worth much more than this, you should consider purchasing an endorsement for electronics. An endorsement typically costs $40-$50 per year.

Floaters

Floaters, on the other hand, extend coverage for a specific item that is very valuable, such as a diamond ring. A floater may even offer coverage if you misplace the item. The cost of a floater depends on the item. A floater for a piece of jewelry appraised at $5,000 may cost about $75 per year.

Depending on the insurance company, endorsements and floaters may offer additional coverage for:

- Sports equipment

- Musical equipment

- Special collections, such as stamp and baseball-card collections

- Boats and watercraft

- Jewelry

- Furs

- Firearms

- Electronics

- Refrigerated property

You may also be able to purchase additional coverage to insure against these perils, which are not covered under standard renters' insurance policies:

- Earthquakes

- Floods

- Sinkholes

- Identity theft

Liability

Most renters' insurance policies offer $100,000 - $300,000 of liability coverage.

If you'd like more than this, you can purchase an umbrella policy to add extra liability coverage. An umbrella policy costs about $250 a year.

An umbrella policy offers liability coverage in addition to that provided by your renters' insurance.

AVAILABLE ADD-ONs

Available Add-Ons	Purpose
Endorsements for jewelry, furs, firearms, and electronics	Increases limits
Floaters	Provides increased limits for appraised personal property such as jewelry, cameras, antiques, musical equipment, electronics, special collections
Identity Theft Restoration	If your identity gets stolen, this coverage can help with cost of legal work, phone calls, and lost wages.
Increased coverage on business property	Protects items you're keeping in your home as business samples or for sale

Separate Policies you can Purchase	Purpose
Personal Umbrella Policy (PUP)	Will protect you if someone sues you over an accident and the amount exceeds the liability limits on renters' insurance
Flood insurance	Your agent can help you purchase a separate policy through the National Flood Insurance plan (NFIP).

Take a Home Inventory

Imagine that all your personal property in your apartment is destroyed. You have renters' insurance, and an insurance agent asks you to make a list of everything that was inside. Could you do it? It would be extremely difficult and you probably wouldn't be able to remember everything. This means that you would not be reimbursed for those items you did not remember to include on your list.

Insurance agents estimate that the average person has $20,000 of personal property—even though it might not seem this way at first.

Before you purchase renters' insurance, walk through your apartment room by room and write down everything you own and estimate how much it would cost to replace it.

Don't forget items that you have stored in a basement, an attic, a garage, or a shed. Take pictures of valuable items or make a video. You walk through each room taking a video with your smart phone or camera, naming items as you go.

Include this information for valuable items:

- Description of the item

- When you purchased the item

- Where you purchased the item

- Serial number/make or model (if applicable)

- Cost to replace the item

The Home Inventory Worksheet on the next page will help you determine how much insurance you need. Be sure to store your inventory list somewhere safe that is not in your apartment, such as in a safety deposit box or a cloud storage box.

Some insurance companies have a "digital online wallet." This is a place where you can store pictures of your property in case your computer is stolen or destroyed. Other insurers have software that you can use to store your list electronically with the insurance company and revise it so that it stays current.

Home Inventory Worksheet

Electronics and Equipment	Description	When Purchased	Where Purchased	Serial#, make/model	Replacement Cost
Television					
DVD Player					
DVDs					
Gaming System					
Camera					
Computer/Laptop					
Printer					
Stereo					
CDs					
Cell Phone					
Washer/Dryer					
Air Conditioner(s)					
Space Heaters					
Fans					
Vacuum Cleaners					
Exercise Equipment					
Humidifier					
Other Items					

Living Room/Den	Description	When Purchased	Where Purchased	Serial#, make/model	Replacement Cost
Carpet/Rugs					
Sofa					
Chairs					
Coffee Table					
End Table					
Desk					
Bookcases					
Books					
Clocks					
Entertainment Center					
Musical Instruments					
Mirrors					

Living Room (con't)	Description	When Purchased	Where Purchased	Serial#, make/model	Replacement Cost
Vases					
Collections (stamps, baseball cards.)					
Lamps					
Pictures/Wall Hangings					
Window Coverings					
Other Items					

Kitchen	Description	When Purchased	Where Purchased	Serial#, make/model	Replacement Cost
Carpet/Rugs					
Window Coverings					
Table					
Chairs					
Refrigerator					
Stove/Oven					
Dishwasher					
Dishes					
Flatware (forks, spoons, etc.)					
Coffee maker					
Toaster					
Microwave					
Lamps					
Pictures/Wall Hangings					
Pots and Pans					
Food/Groceries					
Cleaning Supplies					
Other Items					

Bedroom	Description	When Purchased	Where Purchased	Serial#, make/model	Replacement Cost
Carpet/Rugs					
Window Coverings					
Headboard					
Bed/Mattress					
Linens					
Pillows					
Dresser					
Chest					
Night Tables					
Bookcases					
Books					
Chairs					
Desks					
Mirrors					
Lamps/Light Fixtures					
Pictures/Wall Hangings					
Other Items					

Clothing	Description	When Purchased	Where Purchased	Brand	Replacement Cost
Shoes					
Coats					
Suits					
Dresses					
Jeans/Shorts					
Shirts					
Skirts					
Jewelry					
Other items					

Bathroom	Description	When Purchased	Where Purchased	Serial#, make/model	Replacement Cost
Window Coverings					
Hair Dryers					
Other Electrical Appliances					
Scale					
Shower Curtain					
Towels/Bath Mat					
Pictures/Wall Hangings					
Other items					

Basement & Attic	Description	When Purchased	Where Purchased	Serial#, make/model	Replacement Cost

Garage & Shed	Description	When Purchased	Where Purchased	Serial#, make/model	Replacement Cost

Sports Equipment	Description	When Purchased	Where Purchased	Serial#, make/model	Replacement Cost

Applying for Renters' Insurance

If you own a car, the company that insures your car may offer renters' insurance. Bundling several types of insurance may reduce your cost.

You can also search for companies that offer renters' insurance online. Don't be afraid to apply to more than one company. Choose the company with the best rates for the amount of coverage. Also take into consideration customer reviews and whether the insurance agent was helpful and knowledgeable. You can also research a company's insurance ratings online.

Check the financial strength of the insurance company. This can be an important measure if that company will be able to pay out a claim down the road. Weiss Ratings rates the financial strength of all types of insurance companies so you know you're working with a company with strong financial strength. Visit https://greyhouse.weissratings.com to view ratings for your insurance company.

Ask about an insurance company's claims process—often this can be the deciding factor in choosing a company. Ask the agent to explain how you will be paid if you have a claim.

Some companies give you the funds for the entire claim up front.

Others give you only a fraction of the entire claim and an estimate of the actual cash value (ACV) of your possessions, and then reimburse you for replacement cost after you have purchased new items. If a company pays this way, you must have some significant money saved to replace your items before being reimbursed.

Be aware that there is a difference between an insurance company and an insurance agency. Insurance companies usually have their own insurance agents who sell insurance for that company. An insurance agency also has agents, but the agency offers policies from several insurance companies. So an insurance agent working for an agency can get you quotes from different insurance companies.

The Application

Some companies allow you to complete the application online. Others will email you an application. It usually is not necessary to visit the insurance company in person.

The amount of information required to complete a renters' insurance application varies by insurance company. Some applications are much more detailed than others.

See the sample application on page 25.

In general, however, you will need to provide the following information:

Personal information

- Your name, address, phone number, date of birth, Social Security number, employment status, and marital status

- Do you have a dog that has ever bitten anyone?

- Are there any smokers in your household?

Information about the building

- It is a townhouse, a rented house, an apartment building or a condominium?

- The number of apartments in the building

- The year the building was built (an estimate is usually fine)

- The type of building construction: fire resistive, noncombustible, ordinary, heavy timber, or wood frame

- The type of roof

- Is there a fire hydrant within 1,000 feet?

- Is there a fire station within 5 miles?

Information that can result in a discount on the cost of the policy

- Do you have a smoke detector?

- Do you have a fire alarm?

- Do you have a burglar alarm?

- Do you have a fire extinguisher?

- Do you have deadbolt locks?

- Do you have good credit?

- Does the building have a sprinkler system?

- Does the building have a security system?

- Does the property have a locked gate or a locked entrance?

How Much Coverage Do You Need?

An application for renters' insurance will ask you the following questions:

- How much personal property coverage would you like?

- Do you want replacement cost coverage (RCV) or actual cash value (ACV)?

- How much liability insurance you would like?

- What deductible you would like on the policy?

To determine how much personal property coverage you need, review your home inventory list. Most likely, you will need $20,000 to $50,000 worth of personal property coverage.

Typical liability coverage is usually about $100,000. If you want additional liability coverage, you need to purchase an umbrella policy. If you can afford it, replacement cost coverage is the best option.

You can usually choose to pay in full for the policy or in monthly installments. It's often cheaper to pay in full. If you pay monthly, some companies will require automatic monthly withdrawals from your checking account.

Most companies mail you a policy after you make arrangements for payments. Double-check your policy to make sure you're getting the coverage that you requested.

RENTERS INSURANCE APPLICATION

CLIENT INFORMATION

Name:		Home Phone:	
Insured Address:		Home Fax:	
City:		Work Phone:	
State, Zip:		Work Fax:	
County:		Email:	
Industry/Job Title (h):		Date of Birth	(h) (w)
Industry/Job Title (w):		Children & ages:	
Social Security # (h)			
Social Security # (w)		Referred by:	

BUILDING INFORMATION

Year Built:			
Building Construction:			
Hydrant within 1,000 feet?	Yes ☐ No ☐	Fire station w/in 5 miles?	Yes ☐ No ☐

RATING INFORMATION

Replacement cost of contents:	$	
Limit of Liability requested:	$	$

DISCOUNT INFORMATION

Burglar alarm?	Yes ☐ No ☐	If yes, central off-site monitoring?	Yes ☐ No ☐
Fire alarm?	Yes ☐ No ☐	If yes, central off-site monitoring?	Yes ☐ No ☐
Smoke detectors?	Yes ☐ No ☐	If yes, hard wire connection?	Yes ☐ No ☐
Sprinkler system?	Yes ☐ No ☐	If yes, central off-site monitoring?	Yes ☐ No ☐
Fire extinguisher(s)?	Yes ☐ No ☐	Number of extinguishers:	Yes ☐ No ☐
Fire escape ladder?	Yes ☐ No ☐	Location of ladder:	Yes ☐ No ☐
Security guard patrol/gated community?		Yes ☐ No ☐	
Describe security or community:			
Lightning protection system?	Yes ☐ No ☐	Full time caretaker?	Yes ☐ No ☐
24 hour signal continuity?	Yes ☐ No ☐	Seismic shut-off value?	Yes ☐ No ☐
Power back-up generator?	Yes ☐ No ☐	Temperature monitoring system?	Yes ☐ No ☐
External perimeter protection?	Yes ☐ No ☐	Gas leak detectors?	Yes ☐ No ☐

LOSS INFORMATION

Any losses in the past five years?	Yes ☐ No ☐	If yes, please explain:

SPECIAL COVERAGE INFORMATION

Do you wish to insure any of the following?

Jewelry	Describe	Value $
Furs	Describe	Value $
Guns	Describe	Value $
Fine Arts	Describe	Value $
Silverware	Describe	Value $
Cameras	Describe	Value $
Coin Collection	Describe	Value $
Musical Instruments	Describe	Value $
Wine Collection	Describe	Value $
Sports Memorabilia	Describe	Value $
Other Collectibles	Describe	Value $
Do you have a home safe?		Yes ☐ No ☐
Do you have jewelry in a bank vault?		Yes ☐ No ☐

SPECIAL PROPERTY INFORMATION

Do you own any of the following?

Timeshare	Yes ☐ No ☐	Describe
ATV	Yes ☐ No ☐	Describe
Jet Ski	Yes ☐ No ☐	Describe
Boat/Yacht	Yes ☐ No ☐	Describe
Airplane	Yes ☐ No ☐	Describe
Motorcycle	Yes ☐ No ☐	Describe
Vacation Home	Yes ☐ No ☐	Describe
Mobile Home	Yes ☐ No ☐	Describe
Camper Trailer	Yes ☐ No ☐	Describe
Vehicle Trailer	Yes ☐ No ☐	Describe
Hot Rod/Race Car	Yes ☐ No ☐	Describe
Exotic Care	Yes ☐ No ☐	Describe
Car Club Membership	Yes ☐ No ☐	Describe
Do you participate in "on-track" auto events?	Yes ☐ No ☐	Describe

FLOOD AND EARTHQUAKE INSURANCE OPTION

Your policy does not automatically include Flood or Earthquake Insurance. Do you wish to receive a quote for Flood and/or Earthquake Insurance?   Yes ☐ No ☐

In connection with this application for insurance, the insurer may review your credit report or obtain or use a credit based insurance score based on the information contained in that report. The insurer may use a third party in connection with the development of your insurance score.

Signature_____ Date_____

How to File a Claim

If your personal property is damaged or destroyed and you want reimbursement from the insurance company, you need to contact the insurance company and file a claim.

If the personal property in your apartment is damaged, don't throw anything out. A claims adjuster from the insurance company will want to see the damage.

Taking photos for your records is always a good idea as well.

Get a police report and prepare a list of the damaged items for the claims adjuster. Include receipts whenever possible.

If your apartment is destroyed, you'll need to give the claims adjuster your inventory list with the photographs you took of your property before the incident. If you need to stay at a hotel and eat meals at restaurants, keep all your receipts, so the insurance company can reimburse you.

Description of Perils

Fire or Lightning

Your renters' insurance policy will cover a fire in your apartment or a fire in the building that spreads to your apartment; it will also cover damage caused by a strike of lightning.

Windstorm or Hail

Your policy will cover damage caused by a windstorm or hail if the direct force of the wind of hail damages the building and creates an opening in a wall or the roof allowing rain, sleet, snow, sand, or dust to enter the apartment and damage your personal property.

Explosion

Your insurance company will replace personal property destroyed from an explosion in your apartment or the building.

Riot or Civil Commotion

A riot or civil commotion is a disturbance in public caused by many people. If a riot of civil commotion damages your apartment and your personal property, it will be covered by your renters' insurance.

Aircraft

If an aircraft hits the building and damages your apartment and your personal property, that damage is covered by your renters' insurance. An "aircraft" is a plane or helicopter but it may also be a self-propelled missile or spacecraft.

Vehicles

If a vehicles hits the apartment building and damages your apartment and personal property, that damage is covered by renters' insurance.

Smoke

Sudden and accidental damage caused by smoke, usually from a furnace or a boiler, is covered. "Smoke" refers to smoke, soot, fumes or vapors. It does not include damage from smoke from agricultural or industrial operations.

Vandalism or Malicious Mischief

Vandalism is damage intentionally caused to property. Malicious mischief could mean that damage was accidental. If vandals damage your personal property, it is covered by renters' insurance, but, it may not be covered if your apartment has been vacant—meaning you haven't lived there—for more than 60 days.

Theft

If someone steals your personal property, it is covered by renters' insurance.

Falling Objects

This peril refers to damage caused by a falling object that damages a wall or roof of the building and then damages your personal property. Damage to the falling object itself is not covered.

Weight of Ice, Snow, or Sleet

This peril refers to damage from the weight of ice, snow, or sleet that damages the building and the personal property within it.

Sudden and Accidental Discharge or Overflow of Water or Steam

This applies to water or steam that is discharged from a plumbing, heating, air conditioning, or sprinkler system.

Accidental Tearing Apart, Cracking, Burning, or Bulging

This peril refers to the sudden tearing, cracking, burning, or bulging of a steam or hot-water heating system, an air-conditioning system, or a sprinkler system.

Freezing

Damage caused by freezing of a plumbing, heating, air-conditioning, or sprinkler system.

Sudden and Accidental Damage from Artificially Generated Electrical Current (Power Surges)

This peril does not include loss to the electronic parts of appliances, fixtures, computers, and other types of electronic system.

Volcanic Eruption

This peril includes damage caused by volcanic eruptions, but not earthquakes, land shock waves, or tremors.

Weiss Ratings' Recommended Homeowners Insurers

The following pages list Weiss Ratings' Recommended Homeowners Insurers (based strictly on financial safety) and the states in which they are licensed to do business. Most homeowners insurers also provided renters' insurance policies, so this is a good place to start when selecting a renters' insurance policy. These insurers currently receive a Weiss Safety Rating of A+, A, A-, B+ or B, indicating their strong financial position. Companies are listed by their Safety Rating and then alphabetically within each Safety Rating grouping.

To get Weiss Safety Rating for a company not included here, or to check the latest rating for these companies, go to https://greyhouse.weissratings.com.

Insurer Name

The insurance company's legally registered name, which can sometimes differ from the name that the company uses for advertising. An insurer's name can be very similar to the name of other companies which may not be on this list, so make sure you note the exact name before contacting your agent.

Weiss Safety Rating

Our rating is measured on a scale from A to F and considers a wide range of factors. Highly rated companies are, in our opinion, less likely to experience financial difficulties than lower-rated firms. See "What Our Ratings Mean" in the Appendix for a definition of each rating category.

City & State

The city in which the company's corporate office is located and the state in which the company's corporate office is located.

Licensed In

The states in which an insurer is licensed to conduct business.

Website

The company's web address

Telephone

The telephone number to call for information on purchasing an insurance policy from the company.

The following list of Recommended Homeowners Insurers is based on ratings as of the date of publication. Visit https://greyhouse.weissratings.com to check the latest rating of these companies.

A+ Rated Homeowners Insurers

Insurer:	**CITIZENS PROPERTY INS CORP**
Rating:	A+
Headquarters:	Tallahassee, FL
Licensed In:	FL
Website:	https://www.citizensfla.com
Telephone:	(850) 513-3700

A- Rated Homeowners Insurers

Insurer:	**SELECTIVE CASUALTY INS CO**
Rating:	A-
Headquarters:	Branchville, NJ
Licensed In:	NJ
Website:	https://www.selective.com
Telephone:	(973) 948-3000

B+ Rated Homeowners Insurers

Insurer:	**ALFA ALLIANCE INS CORP**
Rating:	B+
Headquarters:	Glen Allen, VA
Licensed In:	GA, MD, SC, TN, VA
Website:	http://www.alfaaic.com
Telephone:	(804) 346-1900

Insurer:	**ALFA GENERAL INS CORP**
Rating:	B+
Headquarters:	Montgomery, AL
Licensed In:	AL, GA, MS
Website:	https://www.alfainsurance.com
Telephone:	(334) 288-3900

Insurer:	**ALLSTATE INS CO**
Rating:	B+
Headquarters:	Northbrook, IL
Licensed In:	All states except NJ
Website:	http://www.allstate.com
Telephone:	(847) 402-5000

Insurer:	**AMERICAN FAMILY MUTL INS CO SI**
Rating:	B+
Headquarters:	Madison, WI
Licensed In:	AZ, CO, FL, GA, ID, IL, IN, IA, KS, MN, MO, MT, NE, NV, NM, NC, ND, OH, OR, SC, SD, TN, TX, UT, VA, WA, WI, WY
Website:	www.amfam.com
Telephone:	(608) 249-2111

Insurer:	**AMICA MUTUAL INS CO**
Rating:	B+
Headquarters:	Providence, RI
Licensed In:	All states except PR
Website:	https://www.amica.com
Telephone:	(800) 652-6422

Insurer:	**AUTO-OWNERS INS CO**
Rating:	B+
Headquarters:	Lansing, MI
Licensed In:	All states except AK, CA, CT, DC, DE, HI, LA, ME, MD, MA, MT, NH, NJ, NY, OK, RI, TX, VT, WV, WY, PR
Website:	
Telephone:	(517) 323-1200

Insurer:	**CINCINNATI INS CO**
Rating:	B+
Headquarters:	Cincinnati, OH
Licensed In:	All states, the District of Columbia and Puerto Rico
Website:	http://www.cinfin.com
Telephone:	(513) 870-2000

Insurer:	**COUNTRY CASUALTY INS CO**
Rating:	B+
Headquarters:	Bloomington, IL
Licensed In:	All states except CA, DC, FL, HI, LA, MS, NH, NJ, NY, NC, SC, UT, VT, VA, WV, PR
Website:	https://www.countryfinancial.com
Telephone:	(309) 821-3000

Insurer:	**COUNTRY MUTUAL INS CO**
Rating:	B+
Headquarters:	Bloomington, IL
Licensed In:	All states except CA, DC, FL, HI, LA, MS, PR
Website:	https://www.countryfinancial.com
Telephone:	(309) 821-3000

Insurer:	**GARRISON P&C INS CO**
Rating:	B+
Headquarters:	San Antonio, TX
Licensed In:	All states except PR
Website:	https://www.usaa.com
Telephone:	(210) 498-1411

Insurer: **HOME-OWNERS INS CO**
Rating: B+
Headquarters: Lansing, MI
Licensed In: AL, AR, CO, GA, IL, IN, IA, KY, MI, MO, NE, NV, ND, OH, PA, SC, SD, UT, VA, WI
Website: http://www.auto-owners.com
Telephone: (517) 323-1200

Insurer: **INTERINS EXCHANGE**
Rating: B+
Headquarters: Santa Ana, CA
Licensed In: CA, FL, HI, ME, MI, MO, NH, NM, OH, PA, RI, TX, VT, VA
Website: http://www.aaa.com
Telephone: (714) 850-5111

Insurer: **OWNERS INS CO**
Rating: B+
Headquarters: Lansing, MI
Licensed In: All states except AK, CA, CT, DC, DE, HI, LA, ME, MD, MA, MT, NH, NJ, NY, OK, RI, TX, VT, WV, WY, PR
Website: http://www.auto-owners.com
Telephone: (517) 323-1200

Insurer: **PROPERTY-OWNERS INS CO**
Rating: B+
Headquarters: Lansing, MI
Licensed In: AL, AR, GA, IL, IN, IA, KY, MI, MO, NE, NV, ND, SC, SD, UT, VA, WI
Website: http://www.auto-owners.com
Telephone: (517) 323-1200

Insurer: **SELECTIVE F&C INS CO**
Rating: B+
Headquarters: Branchville, NJ
Licensed In: NJ
Website: https://www.selective.com
Telephone: (973) 948-3000

Insurer: **STATE FARM FIRE & CAS CO**
Rating: B+
Headquarters: Bloomington, IL
Licensed In: All states except PR
Website: https://www.statefarm.com
Telephone: (309) 766-2311

Insurer: **TENNESSEE FARMERS MUTUAL INS CO**
Rating: B+
Headquarters: Columbia, TN
Licensed In: TN
Website: https://www.fbitn.com
Telephone: (931) 388-7872

Insurer: **TOKIO MARINE AMERICA INS CO**
Rating: B+
Headquarters: Bala Cynwyd, PA
Licensed In: All states, the District of Columbia and Puerto Rico
Website: HTTP://TMAMERICA.COM
Telephone: (610) 227-1253

Insurer: **TRAVELERS CASUALTY & SURETY CO**
Rating: B+
Headquarters: Hartford, CT
Licensed In: All states, the District of Columbia and Puerto Rico
Website: https://www.travelers.com
Telephone: (860) 277-0111

Insurer: **TRAVELERS INDEMNITY CO**
Rating: B+
Headquarters: Hartford, CT
Licensed In: All states, the District of Columbia and Puerto Rico
Website: https://www.travelers.com
Telephone: (860) 277-0111

Insurer: **UNITED SERVICES AUTOMOBILE ASN**
Rating: B+
Headquarters: San Antonio, TX
Licensed In: All states, the District of Columbia and Puerto Rico
Website: https://www.usaa.com
Telephone: (210) 498-2211

Insurer: **USAA GENERAL INDEMNITY CO**
Rating: B+
Headquarters: San Antonio, TX
Licensed In: All states, the District of Columbia and Puerto Rico
Website: https://www.usaa.com
Telephone: (210) 498-1411

B Rated Homeowners Insurers

Insurer: **ACUITY A MUTUAL INS CO**
Rating: B
Headquarters: Sheboygan, WI
Licensed In: All states except AK, CA, CT, DC, FL, HI, LA, MD, MA, NJ, NY, NC, RI, SC, PR
Website: https://www.acuity.com
Telephone: (920) 458-9131

Insurer: **ALFA INS CORP**
Rating: B
Headquarters: Montgomery, AL
Licensed In: AL, GA, MS
Website: https://www.alfainsurance.com
Telephone: (334) 288-3900

Insurer:	**ALFA MUTUAL GENERAL INS CO**
Rating:	B
Headquarters:	Montgomery, AL
Licensed In:	AL, GA, MS
Website:	https://www.alfainsurance.com
Telephone:	(334) 288-3900

Insurer:	**ALFA MUTUAL INS CO**
Rating:	B
Headquarters:	Montgomery, AL
Licensed In:	AL, FL, GA, IL, IN, KY, NC, OH, PA, VA
Website:	https://www.alfainsurance.com
Telephone:	(334) 288-3900

Insurer:	**ALLSTATE INDEMNITY CO**
Rating:	B
Headquarters:	Northbrook, IL
Licensed In:	All states except NJ, PR
Website:	http://www.allstate.com
Telephone:	(847) 402-5000

Insurer:	**ALLSTATE NJ INS CO**
Rating:	B
Headquarters:	Northbrook, IL
Licensed In:	IL, NJ, PA
Website:	http://www.allstate.com
Telephone:	(908) 252-5000

Insurer:	**ALLSTATE P&C INS CO**
Rating:	B
Headquarters:	Northbrook, IL
Licensed In:	All states except HI, MA, NJ, PR
Website:	http://www.allstate.com
Telephone:	(847) 402-5000

Insurer:	**ALLSTATE TEXAS LLOYDS**
Rating:	B
Headquarters:	Northbrook, IL
Licensed In:	TX
Website:	http://www.allstate.com
Telephone:	(847) 402-5000

Insurer:	**ALLSTATE VEHICLE & PROPERTY INS CO**
Rating:	B
Headquarters:	Northbrook, IL
Licensed In:	All states except CA, NJ, PR
Website:	http://www.allstate.com
Telephone:	(847) 402-5000

Insurer: **AMERICAN BANKERS INS CO OF FL**
Rating: B
Headquarters: Miami, FL
Licensed In: All states, the District of Columbia and Puerto Rico
Website: http://www.assurant.com
Telephone: (305) 253-2244

Insurer: **AMERICAN FAMILY INS CO**
Rating: B
Headquarters: Madison, WI
Licensed In: AZ, CO, GA, ID, IL, IN, IA, KS, MN, MO, NE, NV, ND, OH, OR, SD, UT, WA, WI
Website: https://www.amfam.com
Telephone: (608) 249-2111

Insurer: **AMERICAN HALLMARK INS CO OF TX**
Rating: B
Headquarters: Fort Worth, TX
Licensed In: All states except CA, NH, SD, PR
Website: http://www.hallmarkgrp.com
Telephone: (817) 348-1600

Insurer: **AMERICAN MERCURY INS CO**
Rating: B
Headquarters: Oklahoma City, OK
Licensed In: All states except DC, HI, ME, MA, MI, NH, NY, OH, RI, SC, VT, WV, PR
Website: http://www.mercuryinsurance.com
Telephone: (405) 621-6590

Insurer: **AMERICAN MERCURY LLOYDS INS CO**
Rating: B
Headquarters: Oklahoma City, OK
Licensed In: TX
Website: http://www.mercuryinsurance.com
Telephone: (405) 621-6590

Insurer: **AMERICAN MODERN PROPERTY & CASUALTY**
Rating: B
Headquarters: Cincinnati, OH
Licensed In: All states except FL, NJ, NY, PR
Website: http://www.amig.com
Telephone: (800) 543-2644

Insurer: **AMERICAN NATIONAL GENERAL INS CO**
Rating: B
Headquarters: Springfield, MO
Licensed In: All states except AK, DC, HI, ME, MA, MI, NH, NJ, NY, NC, RI, VT, PR
Website: https://www.americannational.com
Telephone: (417) 887-4990

Insurer: **AMERICAN NATIONAL LLOYDS INS CO**
Rating: B
Headquarters: Springfield, MO
Licensed In: All states except PR
Website: https://www.americannational.com
Telephone: (409) 766-6619

Insurer: **AMERICAN NATIONAL PROPERTY & CAS CO**
Rating: B
Headquarters: Springfield, MO
Licensed In: All states except CT, MA, NY
Website: https://www.americannational.com
Telephone: (417) 887-4990

Insurer: **AMERICAN SECURITY INS CO**
Rating: B
Headquarters: Atlanta, GA
Licensed In: All states except NH
Website:
Telephone: (770) 763-1000

Insurer: **AMERICAN STANDARD INS CO OF OH**
Rating: B
Headquarters: Madison, WI
Licensed In: GA, OH, WI
Website: https://www.amfam.com
Telephone: (608) 249-2111

Insurer: **ANPAC LOUISIANA INS CO**
Rating: B
Headquarters: Springfield, MO
Licensed In: CA, LA, TX
Website: https://www.americannational.com
Telephone: (417) 887-4990

Insurer: **AUTO CLUB INS ASSN**
Rating: B
Headquarters: Dearborn, MI
Licensed In: CA, IL, MI, MN, NE, NY, ND, PA, WI
Website: http://www.aaa.com
Telephone: (313) 336-1234

Insurer: **AUTO CLUB INS CO OF FL**
Rating: B
Headquarters: Tampa, FL
Licensed In: FL
Website: https://www.autoclubfl.com
Telephone: (888) 929-4222

Insurer:	**AUTOMOBILE INS CO OF HARTFORD CT**
Rating:	B
Headquarters:	Hartford, CT
Licensed In:	All states except CA, PR
Website:	https://www.travelers.com
Telephone:	(860) 277-0111

Insurer:	**AXIS INS CO**
Rating:	B
Headquarters:	Alpharetta, GA
Licensed In:	All states except PR
Website:	http://www.axiscapital.com
Telephone:	(678) 746-9400

Insurer:	**BERKLEY INS CO**
Rating:	B
Headquarters:	Greenwich, CT
Licensed In:	All states, the District of Columbia and Puerto Rico
Website:	http://www.wrberkley.com
Telephone:	(203) 542-3800

Insurer:	**CALIFORNIA AUTOMOBILE INS CO**
Rating:	B
Headquarters:	Los Angeles, CA
Licensed In:	CA
Website:	http://www.mercuryinsurance.com
Telephone:	(714) 671-6600

Insurer:	**CANOPIUS US INS INC**
Rating:	B
Headquarters:	Chicago, IL
Licensed In:	All states except PR
Website:	http://www.canopius.com
Telephone:	(630) 994-5600

Insurer:	**CASTLE KEY INDEMNITY CO**
Rating:	B
Headquarters:	Largo, IL
Licensed In:	FL, IL
Website:	http://www.allstate.com
Telephone:	(727) 573-6800

Insurer:	**CASTLE KEY INS CO**
Rating:	B
Headquarters:	Largo, IL
Licensed In:	FL, IL, PA
Website:	http://www.allstate.com
Telephone:	(727) 573-6800

Insurer:	**CENTRAL MUTUAL INS CO**
Rating:	B
Headquarters:	Van Wert, OH
Licensed In:	All states except AL, AK, DC, FL, HI, KS, LA, MO, NE, ND, RI, SD, WV, WY, PR
Website:	www.central-insurance.com
Telephone:	(419) 238-1010

Insurer:	**CHARTER OAK FIRE INS CO**
Rating:	B
Headquarters:	Hartford, CT
Licensed In:	All states except CA
Website:	https://www.travelers.com
Telephone:	(860) 277-0111

Insurer:	**CHUBB INDEMNITY INS CO**
Rating:	B
Headquarters:	Warren, NJ
Licensed In:	All states except PR
Website:	https://www.chubb.com
Telephone:	(215) 640-1000

Insurer:	**CHUBB INS CO OF NJ**
Rating:	B
Headquarters:	Whitehouse Stati, NJ
Licensed In:	NJ
Website:	https://www.chubb.com
Telephone:	(215) 640-1000

Insurer:	**CHUBB LLOYDS INS CO OF TX**
Rating:	B
Headquarters:	Warren, NJ
Licensed In:	MS, TX
Website:	https://www.chubb.com
Telephone:	(215) 640-1000

Insurer:	**CHUBB NATIONAL INS CO**
Rating:	B
Headquarters:	Whitehouse Stati, NJ
Licensed In:	All states except PR
Website:	https://www.chubb.com
Telephone:	(215) 640-1000

Insurer:	**CITIZENS INS CO OF AM**
Rating:	B
Headquarters:	Worcester, MA
Licensed In:	All states except FL, KY, LA, WY, PR
Website:	http://www.hanover.com
Telephone:	(508) 853-7200

Insurer:	**DONEGAL MUTUAL INS CO**
Rating:	B
Headquarters:	Marietta, PA
Licensed In:	AL, CO, DC, DE, GA, IL, IN, IA, ME, MD, MI, NE, NH, NM, NC, OH, OK, PA, SC, SD, TN, TX, UT, VT, VA, WV, WI
Website:	https://www.donegalgroup.com
Telephone:	(717) 426-1931

Insurer:	**ECONOMY PREMIER ASR CO**
Rating:	B
Headquarters:	Warwick, RI
Licensed In:	All states except AK, CA, DC, DE, HI, ME, MA, MI, NV, NH, NJ, RI, SC, VT, PR
Website:	https://www.metlife.com
Telephone:	(401) 827-2400

Insurer:	**ENCOMPASS INDEMNITY CO**
Rating:	B
Headquarters:	Northbrook, IL
Licensed In:	All states except CA, FL, HI, ME, MA, NJ, PR
Website:	http://www.encompassinsurance.com
Telephone:	(847) 402-5000

Insurer:	**ERIE INS EXCHANGE**
Rating:	B
Headquarters:	Erie, PA
Licensed In:	All states except AK, AZ, AR, CA, CO, FL, HI, ID, KS, LA, MA, MI, MS, OK, OR, UT, WA, PR
Website:	https://www.erieinsurance.com
Telephone:	(814) 870-2000

Insurer:	**EXECUTIVE RISK INDEMNITY INC**
Rating:	B
Headquarters:	Whitehouse Stati, NJ
Licensed In:	All states except PR
Website:	
Telephone:	(215) 640-1000

Insurer:	**FARM BU TOWN & COUNTRY INS CO OF MO**
Rating:	B
Headquarters:	Jefferson City, MO
Licensed In:	MO
Website:	https://www.mofbinsurance.com
Telephone:	(573) 893-1400

Insurer:	**FARM BUREAU GENERAL INS CO OF MI**
Rating:	B
Headquarters:	Lansing, MI
Licensed In:	MI
Website:	https://www.farmbureauinsurance-mi.com
Telephone:	(517) 323-7000

Insurer: **FARM BUREAU MUTUAL INS CO OF AR**
Rating: B
Headquarters: Little Rock, AR
Licensed In: AR
Website: https://afbic.com
Telephone: (501) 224-4400

Insurer: **FARM BUREAU P&C INS CO**
Rating: B
Headquarters: West Des Moines, IA
Licensed In: AZ, ID, IA, KS, MN, MO, NE, NM, SD, UT, WI
Website: https://www.fbfs.com
Telephone: (515) 225-5400

Insurer: **FARM FAMILY CASUALTY INS CO**
Rating: B
Headquarters: Albany, NY
Licensed In: CT, DE, ME, MD, MA, MO, NH, NJ, NY, PA, RI, VT, VA, WV
Website: https://www.americannational.com
Telephone: (518) 431-5000

Insurer: **FARMERS AUTOMOBILE INS ASN**
Rating: B
Headquarters: Pekin, IL
Licensed In: AZ, IL, IN, IA, MI, OH, UT, WI
Website: http://www.pekininsurance.com
Telephone: (309) 346-1161

Insurer: **FARMERS INS CO OF FLEMINGTON**
Rating: B
Headquarters: Flemington, NJ
Licensed In: NJ
Website: http://www.farmersofflemington.com
Telephone: (908) 782-4120

Insurer: **FARMERS INS CO OF OREGON**
Rating: B
Headquarters: Tigard, OR
Licensed In: CA, MI, OR
Website: https://www.farmers.com
Telephone: (503) 686-6114

Insurer: **FARMERS MUTUAL INS CO OF NE**
Rating: B
Headquarters: Lincoln, NE
Licensed In: IL, IN, IA, KS, NE, ND, SD
Website: www.fmne.com
Telephone: (402) 434-8300

Insurer:	**FARMINGTON CASUALTY CO**
Rating:	B
Headquarters:	Hartford, CT
Licensed In:	All states except PR
Website:	https://www.travelers.com
Telephone:	(860) 277-0111

Insurer:	**FEDERATED MUTUAL INS CO**
Rating:	B
Headquarters:	Owatonna, MN
Licensed In:	All states except HI, PR
Website:	https://www.federatedinsurance.com
Telephone:	(507) 455-5200

Insurer:	**FIRST FLORIDIAN AUTO & HOME INS CO**
Rating:	B
Headquarters:	Tampa, FL
Licensed In:	FL
Website:	https://www.travelers.com
Telephone:	(813) 357-0200

Insurer:	**FOREMOST INS CO**
Rating:	B
Headquarters:	Grand Rapids, MI
Licensed In:	All states except PR
Website:	http://www.foremost.com
Telephone:	(616) 942-3000

Insurer:	**FRANKENMUTH MUTUAL INS CO**
Rating:	B
Headquarters:	Frankenmuth, MI
Licensed In:	All states except AK, CA, HI, PR
Website:	www.fmins.com
Telephone:	(989) 652-6121

Insurer:	**GRANGE MUTUAL CAS CO**
Rating:	B
Headquarters:	Columbus, OH
Licensed In:	AL, GA, IL, IN, IA, KS, KY, MN, MO, OH, PA, SC, TN, VA, WI
Website:	www.grangeinsurance.com
Telephone:	(614) 445-2900

Insurer:	**GREAT NORTHERN INS CO**
Rating:	B
Headquarters:	Whitehouse Stati, NJ
Licensed In:	All states except PR
Website:	https://www.chubb.com
Telephone:	(215) 640-1000

Insurer:	**HARTFORD ACCIDENT & INDEMNITY CO**
Rating:	B
Headquarters:	Hartford, CT
Licensed In:	All states except PR
Website:	http://www.thehartford.com
Telephone:	(860) 547-5000

Insurer:	**HARTFORD CASUALTY INS CO**
Rating:	B
Headquarters:	Hartford, CT
Licensed In:	All states except PR
Website:	http://www.thehartford.com
Telephone:	(860) 547-5000

Insurer:	**HARTFORD INS CO OF IL**
Rating:	B
Headquarters:	Hartford, CT
Licensed In:	AZ, CT, HI, IL, MI, NY, NC, PA
Website:	http://www.thehartford.com
Telephone:	(860) 547-5000

Insurer:	**HARTFORD INS CO OF THE MIDWEST**
Rating:	B
Headquarters:	Hartford, CT
Licensed In:	All states except PR
Website:	http://www.thehartford.com
Telephone:	(860) 547-5000

Insurer:	**HARTFORD INS CO OF THE SOUTHEAST**
Rating:	B
Headquarters:	Hartford, CT
Licensed In:	AZ, CT, FL, GA, IL, KS, LA, MI, NC, PA
Website:	http://www.thehartford.com
Telephone:	(860) 547-5000

Insurer:	**HARTFORD LLOYDS INS CO**
Rating:	B
Headquarters:	Hartford, CT
Licensed In:	TX
Website:	http://www.thehartford.com
Telephone:	(860) 547-5000

Insurer:	**HARTFORD UNDERWRITERS INS CO**
Rating:	B
Headquarters:	Hartford, CT
Licensed In:	All states except PR
Website:	http://www.thehartford.com
Telephone:	(860) 547-5000

Insurer:	**HASTINGS MUTUAL INS CO**
Rating:	B
Headquarters:	Hastings, MI
Licensed In:	IL, IN, IA, KY, MI, OH, PA, TN, WI
Website:	www.hastingsmutual.com
Telephone:	(800) 442-8277

Insurer:	**HIGH POINT PREFERRED INS CO**
Rating:	B
Headquarters:	Lincroft, NJ
Licensed In:	NJ, PA
Website:	https://www.plymouthrock.com
Telephone:	(732) 978-6000

Insurer:	**HORACE MANN INS CO**
Rating:	B
Headquarters:	Springfield, IL
Licensed In:	All states except HI, NJ, PR
Website:	http://www.horacemann.com
Telephone:	(217) 789-2500

Insurer:	**HORACE MANN P&C INS CO**
Rating:	B
Headquarters:	Springfield, IL
Licensed In:	All states except HI, MA, NJ, PR
Website:	http://www.horacemann.com
Telephone:	(217) 789-2500

Insurer:	**IDS PROPERTY CASUALTY INS CO**
Rating:	B
Headquarters:	Green Bay, WI
Licensed In:	All states except PR
Website:	https://www.ameriprise.com
Telephone:	(920) 330-5100

Insurer:	**IMT INS CO**
Rating:	B
Headquarters:	Des Moines, IA
Licensed In:	AZ, IL, IN, IA, MN, MO, NE, ND, SD, WI
Website:	https://www.imtins.com
Telephone:	(515) 453-0777

Insurer:	**INDIANA FARMERS MUTUAL INS CO**
Rating:	B
Headquarters:	Indianapolis, IN
Licensed In:	IL, IN, KY, OH, TN
Website:	http://insurance.indianafarmers.com
Telephone:	(317) 846-4211

Insurer: **INTEGRITY MUTUAL INS CO**
Rating: B
Headquarters: Appleton, WI
Licensed In: IL, IA, MN, OH, WI
Website: https://www.integrityinsurance.com
Telephone: (920) 734-4511

Insurer: **KEMPER INDEPENDENCE INS CO**
Rating: B
Headquarters: Jacksonville, FL
Licensed In: AZ, CA, CO, CT, GA, IL, IN, KS, ME, MD, MI, MO, NV, NY, NC, OH, OR, PA, SD, TX, VT, VA, WI
Website: http://www.kemper.com
Telephone: (904) 245-5600

Insurer: **KINSALE INS CO**
Rating: B
Headquarters: Richmond, VA
Licensed In: All states, the District of Columbia and Puerto Rico
Website: http://www.kinsaleins.com
Telephone: (804) 289-1300

Insurer: **LIBERTY MUTUAL INS CO**
Rating: B
Headquarters: Boston, MA
Licensed In: All states, the District of Columbia and Puerto Rico
Website: https://www.libertymutual.com
Telephone: (617) 357-9500

Insurer: **MERCURY CASUALTY CO**
Rating: B
Headquarters: Los Angeles, CA
Licensed In: AZ, CA, FL, GA, IL, MI, NV, NJ, NY, OK, PA, TX, VA, WA
Website: http://www.mercuryinsurance.com
Telephone: (714) 671-6600

Insurer: **MERCURY INS CO OF GA**
Rating: B
Headquarters: Atlanta, GA
Licensed In: GA
Website: http://www.mercuryinsurance.com
Telephone: (770) 552-5100

Insurer: **MERCURY INS CO OF IL**
Rating: B
Headquarters: Vernon Hills, IL
Licensed In: IL, NJ, PA
Website: http://www.mercuryinsurance.com
Telephone: (847) 816-4300

Insurer: **MET LLOYDS INS CO OF TX**
Rating: B
Headquarters: Warwick, RI
Licensed In: TX
Website: https://www.metlife.com
Telephone: (401) 827-2400

Insurer: **METROPOLITAN DIRECT PROP & CAS INS**
Rating: B
Headquarters: Warwick, RI
Licensed In: All states except MA, MN, VT, WY, PR
Website: https://www.metlife.com
Telephone: (401) 827-2400

Insurer: **METROPOLITAN GROUP PROP & CAS INS CO**
Rating: B
Headquarters: Warwick, RI
Licensed In: All states except HI, KY, ME, MN, NM, NC, OR, VA, WY, PR
Website: https://www.metlife.com
Telephone: (401) 827-2400

Insurer: **MID-CENTURY INS CO**
Rating: B
Headquarters: Los Angeles, CA
Licensed In: All states except AK, ME, PR
Website: https://www.farmers.com
Telephone: (323) 932-3200

Insurer: **MOTOR CLUB INS CO**
Rating: B
Headquarters: Costa Mesa, CA
Licensed In: RI
Website:
Telephone: (714) 850-5111

Insurer: **MUTUAL OF ENUMCLAW INS CO**
Rating: B
Headquarters: Enumclaw, WA
Licensed In: AK, AZ, CO, ID, MT, NV, NM, OR, UT, WA
Website: http://www.mutualofenumclaw.com
Telephone: (360) 825-2591

Insurer: **NATIONWIDE AFFINITY INS CO OF AMER**
Rating: B
Headquarters: Columbus, OH
Licensed In: All states except AR, CA, HI, MI, PR
Website: https://www.nationwide.com
Telephone: (614) 249-7111

Insurer: **NATIONWIDE INS CO OF FL**
Rating: B
Headquarters: Columbus, OH
Licensed In: FL, OH
Website: https://www.nationwide.com
Telephone: (614) 249-7111

Insurer: **NATIONWIDE MUTUAL INS CO**
Rating: B
Headquarters: Columbus, OH
Licensed In: All states except PR
Website: https://www.nationwide.com
Telephone: (614) 249-7111

Insurer: **NJ MANUFACTURERS INS CO**
Rating: B
Headquarters: West Trenton, NJ
Licensed In: CT, DE, ME, MD, NJ, NY, PA, RI
Website: http://www.njm.com
Telephone: (609) 883-1300

Insurer: **NORTH CAROLINA FARM BU MUTUAL INS CO**
Rating: B
Headquarters: Raleigh, NC
Licensed In: NC
Website: http://www.ncfbins.com
Telephone: (919) 782-1705

Insurer: **NORTH LIGHT SPECIALTY INS CO**
Rating: B
Headquarters: Northbrook, IL
Licensed In: All states except DC, NE, NM, SD, WY, PR
Website: https://www.northlightspecialty.com
Telephone: (847) 402-5000

Insurer: **P&C INS CO OF HARTFORD**
Rating: B
Headquarters: Hartford, CT
Licensed In: All states except HI, NH, PR
Website: http://www.thehartford.com
Telephone: (860) 547-5000

Insurer: **PACIFIC INDEMNITY CO**
Rating: B
Headquarters: Whitehouse Stati, NJ
Licensed In: All states except PR
Website: https://www.chubb.com
Telephone: (215) 640-1000

Insurer: **PEERLESS INS CO**
Rating: B
Headquarters: Boston, MA
Licensed In: All states except HI, PR
Website: https://www.peerless-ins.com
Telephone: (617) 357-9500

Insurer: **PEKIN INS CO**
Rating: B
Headquarters: Pekin, IL
Licensed In: AZ, IL, IN, IA, MI, OH, UT, WI
Website: http://www.pekininsurance.com
Telephone: (309) 346-1161

Insurer: **PHOENIX INS CO**
Rating: B
Headquarters: Hartford, CT
Licensed In: All states except CA, PR
Website: https://www.travelers.com
Telephone: (860) 277-0111

Insurer: **PIONEER STATE MUTUAL INS CO**
Rating: B
Headquarters: Flint, MI
Licensed In: IN, MI
Website: https://www.psmic.com
Telephone: (810) 733-2300

Insurer: **PREFERRED MUTUAL INS CO**
Rating: B
Headquarters: New Berlin, NY
Licensed In: CT, MA, NH, NJ, NY, NC, OH, PA, RI, SC
Website: https://www.preferredmutual.com
Telephone: (607) 847-6161

Insurer: **PRIVILEGE UNDERWRITERS RECIP EXCH**
Rating: B
Headquarters: White Plains, NY
Licensed In: All states except ID, PR
Website: http://www.pureinsurance.com
Telephone: (914) 328-7388

Insurer: **PROVIDENCE MUTUAL FIRE INS CO**
Rating: B
Headquarters: Providence, RI
Licensed In: CT, ME, MA, NH, NJ, NY, RI, VT
Website: http://www.providencemutual.com
Telephone: (401) 827-1800

Insurer:	**QBE INS CORP**
Rating:	B
Headquarters:	New York, NY
Licensed In:	All states except PR
Website:	
Telephone:	(608) 825-5160

Insurer:	**RLI INS CO**
Rating:	B
Headquarters:	Peoria, IL
Licensed In:	All states, the District of Columbia and Puerto Rico
Website:	https://www.rlicorp.com
Telephone:	(309) 692-1000

Insurer:	**SAFECO INS CO OF AMERICA**
Rating:	B
Headquarters:	Boston, MA
Licensed In:	All states except PR
Website:	http://www.safeco.com
Telephone:	(617) 357-9500

Insurer:	**SAFECO INS CO OF IL**
Rating:	B
Headquarters:	Boston, MA
Licensed In:	All states except DC, DE, HI, ME, MA, NH, NJ, NY, NC, ND, RI, SC, SD, VT, WV, PR
Website:	http://www.safeco.com
Telephone:	(617) 357-9500

Insurer:	**SAFECO INS CO OF INDIANA**
Rating:	B
Headquarters:	Boston, MA
Licensed In:	All states except CA, FL, ME, MI, NH, PR
Website:	http://www.safeco.com
Telephone:	(617) 357-9500

Insurer:	**SAFECO INS CO OF OREGON**
Rating:	B
Headquarters:	Boston, MA
Licensed In:	GA, LA, OR, WA
Website:	http://www.safeco.com
Telephone:	(617) 357-9500

Insurer:	**SELECTIVE AUTO INS CO OF NJ**
Rating:	B
Headquarters:	Branchville, NJ
Licensed In:	NJ, NC
Website:	https://www.selective.com
Telephone:	(973) 948-3000

Insurer: **SELECTIVE INS CO OF SC**
Rating: B
Headquarters: Branchville, NJ
Licensed In: All states except AK, AR, CA, DC, FL, HI, ID, LA, ME, MT, NE, NV, ND, OK, OR, TX, WY, PR
Website: https://www.selective.com
Telephone: (973) 948-3000

Insurer: **SELECTIVE INS CO OF THE SOUTHEAST**
Rating: B
Headquarters: Branchville, NJ
Licensed In: All states except AK, AR, CA, HI, ID, ME, MT, NE, ND, OR, WY, PR
Website: https://www.selective.com
Telephone: (973) 948-3000

Insurer: **SENTINEL INS CO LTD**
Rating: B
Headquarters: Hartford, CT
Licensed In: All states except PR
Website: http://www.thehartford.com
Telephone: (860) 547-5000

Insurer: **SHELTER MUTUAL INS CO**
Rating: B
Headquarters: Columbia, MO
Licensed In: All states except AK, AZ, CA, CT, DC, FL, HI, ME, MI, NM, ND, RI, UT, WA, PR
Website: https://www.shelterinsurance.com
Telephone: (573) 445-8441

Insurer: **SOUTHERN-OWNERS INS CO**
Rating: B
Headquarters: Lansing, MI
Licensed In: FL, MI
Website: http://www.auto-owners.com
Telephone: (517) 323-1200

Insurer: **STANDARD FIRE INS CO**
Rating: B
Headquarters: Hartford, CT
Licensed In: All states except PR
Website: https://www.travelers.com
Telephone: (860) 277-0111

Insurer: **STATE FARM LLOYDS**
Rating: B
Headquarters: Dallas, TX
Licensed In: TX
Website: https://www.statefarm.com
Telephone: (972) 732-5000

Insurer: **TEACHERS INS CO**
Rating: B
Headquarters: Springfield, IL
Licensed In: All states except CA, HI, NJ, PR
Website: http://www.horacemann.com
Telephone: (217) 789-2500

Insurer: **TRAVCO INS CO**
Rating: B
Headquarters: Hartford, CT
Licensed In: All states except AK, CA, PR
Website: https://www.travelers.com
Telephone: (860) 277-0111

Insurer: **TRAVELERS COMMERCIAL INS CO**
Rating: B
Headquarters: Hartford, CT
Licensed In: All states except HI, NH, PR
Website: https://www.travelers.com
Telephone: (860) 277-0111

Insurer: **TRAVELERS HOME & MARINE INS CO**
Rating: B
Headquarters: Hartford, CT
Licensed In: All states except AK, CA, PR
Website: https://www.travelers.com
Telephone: (860) 277-0111

Insurer: **TRAVELERS INDEMNITY CO OF AMERICA**
Rating: B
Headquarters: Hartford, CT
Licensed In: All states except CA, PR
Website: https://www.travelers.com
Telephone: (860) 277-0111

Insurer: **TRAVELERS INDEMNITY CO OF CT**
Rating: B
Headquarters: Hartford, CT
Licensed In: All states, the District of Columbia and Puerto Rico
Website: https://www.travelers.com
Telephone: (860) 277-0111

Insurer: **TRAVELERS LLOYDS OF TEXAS INS CO**
Rating: B
Headquarters: Hartford, CT
Licensed In: TX
Website: https://www.travelers.com
Telephone: (860) 277-0111

Insurer: **TRAVELERS PERSONAL INS CO**
Rating: B
Headquarters: Hartford, CT
Licensed In: All states except AK, CA, FL, HI, ID, LA, MI, NV, ND, SD, WV, WY, PR
Website: https://www.travelers.com
Telephone: (860) 277-0111

Insurer: **TRAVELERS PERSONAL SECURITY INS CO**
Rating: B
Headquarters: Hartford, CT
Licensed In: All states except AK, CA, FL, HI, ID, LA, MN, NV, ND, SD, WV, WY, PR
Website: https://www.travelers.com
Telephone: (860) 277-0111

Insurer: **TRAVELERS PROPERTY CAS OF AMERICA**
Rating: B
Headquarters: Hartford, CT
Licensed In: All states, the District of Columbia and Puerto Rico
Website: https://www.travelers.com
Telephone: (860) 277-0111

Insurer: **TRAVELERS PROPERTY CASUALTY INS CO**
Rating: B
Headquarters: Hartford, CT
Licensed In: All states except HI, MA, NH, PR
Website: https://www.travelers.com
Telephone: (860) 277-0111

Insurer: **TRUMBULL INS CO**
Rating: B
Headquarters: Hartford, CT
Licensed In: All states except HI, PR
Website: http://www.thehartford.com
Telephone: (860) 547-5000

Insurer: **TWIN CITY FIRE INS CO**
Rating: B
Headquarters: Hartford, CT
Licensed In: All states except PR
Website: http://www.thehartford.com
Telephone: (860) 547-5000

Insurer: **UFB CASUALTY INS CO**
Rating: B
Headquarters: Indianapolis, IN
Licensed In: IN
Website: https://www.infarmbureau.com
Telephone: (317) 692-7200

Insurer:	**UNITED FARM FAMILY INS CO**
Rating:	B
Headquarters:	Albany, NY
Licensed In:	DE, MD, NJ, NY, PA, VT, WV
Website:	https://www.americannational.com
Telephone:	(518) 431-5000

Insurer:	**UNITED FARM FAMILY MUTUAL INS CO**
Rating:	B
Headquarters:	Indianapolis, IN
Licensed In:	IN, OH
Website:	https://www.infarmbureau.com
Telephone:	(317) 692-7200

Insurer:	**UNITED FIRE & CAS CO**
Rating:	B
Headquarters:	Cedar Rapids, IA
Licensed In:	All states except DE, NH, PR
Website:	
Telephone:	(319) 399-5700

Insurer:	**UNITED SPECIALTY INS CO**
Rating:	B
Headquarters:	Fort Worth, TX
Licensed In:	All states except PR
Website:	http://www.statenational.com
Telephone:	(817) 265-2000

Insurer:	**UNITRIN DIRECT PROPERTY & CAS CO**
Rating:	B
Headquarters:	Vista, CA
Licensed In:	All states except AK, DC, DE, HI, ID, IA, ME, MA, MT, NE, NH, NJ, NM, ND, RI, SD, VT, WV, WY, PR
Website:	http://www.kemper.com
Telephone:	(312) 661-4600

Insurer:	**UNITRIN SAFEGUARD INS CO**
Rating:	B
Headquarters:	Brookfield, WI
Licensed In:	All states except AK, CA, CT, FL, HI, MA, MI, NH, NJ, RI, WA, PR
Website:	http://www.kemper.com
Telephone:	(904) 245-5600

Insurer:	**USAA CASUALTY INS CO**
Rating:	B
Headquarters:	San Antonio, TX
Licensed In:	All states except PR
Website:	https://www.usaa.com
Telephone:	(210) 498-1411

Insurer:	**VALLEY P&C INS CO**
Rating:	B
Headquarters:	Salem, OR
Licensed In:	OR, WA, WI
Website:	http://www.kemper.com
Telephone:	(904) 245-5600

Insurer:	**VAULT E&S INSURANCE CO**
Rating:	B
Headquarters:	New York, NY
Licensed In:	All states except IN, IA, MN, NE, NY, OR, PR
Website:	www.vault.insurance
Telephone:	(646) 794-0500

Insurer:	**VAULT RECIPROCAL EXCHANGE**
Rating:	B
Headquarters:	New York, NY
Licensed In:	AK, AZ, AR, CT, FL, IN, LA, MI, NH, NM, NC, ND, OK, PA, SC, UT, VT, WV
Website:	http://www.vault.insurance
Telephone:	(646) 794-0500

Insurer:	**VIGILANT INS CO**
Rating:	B
Headquarters:	Warren, NJ
Licensed In:	All states except PR
Website:	https://www.chubb.com
Telephone:	(215) 640-1000

Insurer:	**WAWANESA GENERAL INS CO**
Rating:	B
Headquarters:	San Diego, CA
Licensed In:	CA, OR
Website:	http://www.wawanesa.com/us/california/index.html
Telephone:	(858) 874-5421

Insurer:	**WEST BEND MUTUAL INS CO**
Rating:	B
Headquarters:	West Bend, WI
Licensed In:	AK, AZ, AR, IL, IN, IA, KS, KY, MI, MN, MO, NE, NC, OH, OK, PA, SC, SD, TN, TX, UT, VT, WI
Website:	www.thesilverlining.com
Telephone:	(262) 334-5571

Insurer:	**WESTERN AGRICULTURAL INS CO**
Rating:	B
Headquarters:	West Des Moines, IA
Licensed In:	AL, AZ, AR, CO, ID, IL, IN, IA, KS, MI, MN, MO, MT, NE, NV, NM, ND, OH, OK, SC, SD, TN, TX, UT, VA, WI, WY
Website:	https://www.fbfs.com
Telephone:	(515) 225-5400

Insurer:	**WILSON MUTUAL INS CO**
Rating:	B
Headquarters:	Columbus, OH
Licensed In:	MN, OH, WI
Website:	HTTPS://WWW.MOTORISTSINSURANCEGROUP.COM/WHO-WE-A
Telephone:	(614) 225-8211

Insurer:	**ZURICH AMERICAN INS CO**
Rating:	B
Headquarters:	Schaumburg, IL
Licensed In:	All states, the District of Columbia and Puerto Rico
Website:	www.zurichna.com
Telephone:	(847) 605-6000

Weiss Ratings' Weakest Homeowners Insurers

The following pages list Weiss Ratings' Weakest Homeowners Insurers (based strictly on financial safety) licensed to do business in each state. These insurers currently receive a Weiss Safety Rating of D, D-, E+, E, or E-, indicating their weak financial position.

The company currently demonstrates what we consider to be significant weaknesses and has also failed some of the basic tests that we use to identify fiscal stability. Therefore, even in a favorable economic environment, it is our opinion that policyholders could incur significant risks.

Companies are listed by their Safety Rating and then alphabetically within each Safety Rating grouping.

To get Weiss Safety Rating for a company not included here, or to check the latest rating for these companies, go to https://greyhouse.weissratings.com.

Insurer Name	The insurance company's legally registered name, which can sometimes differ from the name that the company uses for advertising. An insurer's name can be very similar to the name of other companies which may not be on this list, so make sure you note the exact name before contacting your agent.
Weiss Safety Rating	Our rating is measured on a scale from A to F and considers a wide range of factors. Highly rated companies are, in our opinion, less likely to experience financial difficulties than lower-rated firms. See "What Our Ratings Mean" in the Appendix for a definition of each rating category.
City & State	The city in which the company's corporate office is located and the state in which the company's corporate office is located.
Licensed In	The states in which an insurer is licensed to conduct business.
Website	The company's web address
Telephone	The telephone number to call for information on purchasing an insurance policy from the company.

The following list of Weakest Homeowners Insurers is based on ratings as of the date of publication. Visit https://greyhouse.weissratings.com to check the latest rating of these companies.

E- Rated Homeowners Insurers

Insurer:	**KENSINGTON INS CO**
Rating:	E-
Headquarters:	New York, NY
Licensed In:	NY
Website:	http://www.kensington-ins.com
Telephone:	(212) 629-8838

E Rated Homeowners Insurers

Insurer:	**INTEGRITY SELECT INSURANCE CO**
Rating:	E
Headquarters:	Appleton, WI
Licensed In:	IA, MN, OH, WI
Website:	https://www.integrityinsurance.com
Telephone:	(920) 734-4511

Insurer:	**MT MORRIS MUTUAL INS CO**
Rating:	E
Headquarters:	Coloma, WI
Licensed In:	WI
Website:	http://www.mtmorrisins.com
Telephone:	(715) 228-5541

Insurer:	**SOMPO JAPAN NIPPONKOA INS INC**
Rating:	E
Headquarters:	Tamuning, GU
Licensed In:	No States
Website:	http://guahaninsurance.com
Telephone:	(671) 475-4730

Insurer:	**TEXAS FAIR PLAN ASSN**
Rating:	E
Headquarters:	Austin, TX
Licensed In:	TX
Website:	https://www.texasfairplan.org
Telephone:	(512) 899-4900

E+ Rated Homeowners Insurers

Insurer: **UNDERWRITERS AT LLOYDS (VI)**
Rating: E+
Headquarters: Frankfort, KY
Licensed In: No States
Website: http://www.lloyds.com
Telephone: (502) 875-5940

Insurer: **UNITED HERITAGE PROP & CAS CO**
Rating: E+
Headquarters: Meridian, ID
Licensed In: AZ, ID, OR, UT, WA
Website: https://www.unitedheritagepc.com
Telephone: (800) 657-6351

D- Rated Homeowners Insurers

Insurer: **AVATAR P&C INS CO**
Rating: D-
Headquarters: Tampa, FL
Licensed In: FL
Website: http://www.avatarins.com
Telephone: (813) 514-0333

Insurer: **DB INS CO LTD (US BRANCH)**
Rating: D-
Headquarters: Honolulu, HI
Licensed In: CA, HI, IN, NY, OH
Website: www.dbinsus.com
Telephone: (808) 942-5353

Insurer: **FARMERS MUTUAL INS CO OF MI**
Rating: D-
Headquarters: Coldwater, MI
Licensed In: MI
Website: http://www.fmibc.com
Telephone: (517) 278-2108

Insurer: **LEMONADE INS CO**
Rating: D-
Headquarters: New York, NY
Licensed In: All states except AL, AK, CO, DE, FL, HI, ID, KS, KY, ME, MA, MN, MS, NH, SC, SD, TN, UT, VT, WA, WV, WY, PR
Website: http://www.lemonade.com
Telephone: (844) 733-8666

D Rated Homeowners Insurers

Insurer: **ANCHOR P&C INS CO**
Rating: D
Headquarters: Saint Petersburg, FL
Licensed In: FL
Website: http://www.relyonanchor.com
Telephone: (727) 853-6670

Insurer: **ARIZONA HOME INS CO**
Rating: D
Headquarters: Scottsdale, AZ
Licensed In: AZ
Website: http://www.arizonahomeinsurance.com
Telephone: (949) 724-9402

Insurer: **CONIFER INS CO**
Rating: D
Headquarters: Southfield, MI
Licensed In: All states except NY, PR
Website: http://www.coniferinsurance.com
Telephone: (248) 559-0840

Insurer: **EDISON INS CO**
Rating: D
Headquarters: Boca Raton, FL
Licensed In: FL, NJ
Website: http://www.edisoninsurance.com
Telephone: (866) 568-8922

Insurer: **EXCALIBUR NATIONAL INS CO**
Rating: D
Headquarters: Slidell, LA
Licensed In: LA
Website:
Telephone: (985) 781-1444

Insurer: **FARMERS UNION MUTUAL INS CO**
Rating: D
Headquarters: Bryant, AR
Licensed In: AR
Website: http://www.farmersunionmutual.net
Telephone: (501) 847-1518

Insurer: **FARMINGTON MUTUAL INS CO**
Rating: D
Headquarters: Medford, WI
Licensed In: WI
Website: https://www.littleblackmutual.com
Telephone: (715) 748-6040

Insurer: **FLORIDA SPECIALTY INS CO**
Rating: D
Headquarters: Sarasota, FL
Licensed In: AZ, FL, NE
Website: http://floridaspecialty.com
Telephone: (941) 210-5670

Insurer: **FREMONT INS CO**
Rating: D
Headquarters: Fremont, MI
Licensed In: IN, IA, MI, WI
Website: https://www.fmic.com
Telephone: (231) 924-0300

Insurer: **FULMONT MUTUAL INS CO**
Rating: D
Headquarters: Johnstown, NY
Licensed In: NY
Website:
Telephone: (518) 762-3171

Insurer: **MOUNTAIN VALLEY INDEMNITY CO**
Rating: D
Headquarters: Winston-Salem, NC
Licensed In: CO, DE, HI, ID, IN, KS, KY, ME, MD, MA, MO, MT, NE, NV, NH, NY, OK, OR, PA, RI, SC, TN, TX, UT, VT, WA
Website: http://www.mvic-aie.com
Telephone: (336) 435-2000

Insurer: **NEW JERSEY SKYLANDS INS ASSN**
Rating: D
Headquarters: New York, NY
Licensed In: NJ
Website: http://www.njsi.com
Telephone: (336) 435-2000

Insurer: **OTSEGO COUNTY PATRONS CO-OP F R ASN**
Rating: D
Headquarters: Schenevus, NY
Licensed In: NY
Website:
Telephone: (607) 638-9741

Insurer: **PALISADES P&C INS CO**
Rating: D
Headquarters: Woodbridge, NJ
Licensed In: NJ, PA
Website: https://www.plymouthrock.com
Telephone: (732) 978-6000

Insurer: **PALOMAR SPECIALTY INS CO**
Rating: D
Headquarters: La Jolla, CA
Licensed In: AL, AK, AZ, AR, CA, GA, HI, IL, IN, KS, KY, LA, MS, MO, NV, NC, OK, OR, PA, SC, TN, TX, UT, WA
Website: palomarspecialty.com
Telephone: (619) 567-5290

Insurer: **SOUTHERN FIDELITY P&C INC**
Rating: D
Headquarters: Tallahassee, FL
Licensed In: AL, FL, SC
Website: https://www.southernfidelityins.com
Telephone: (850) 521-3080

Insurer: **ST JOHNS INS CO**
Rating: D
Headquarters: Orlando, FL
Licensed In: FL, SC
Website: http://www.stjohnsinsurance.com
Telephone: (407) 226-8460

Insurer: **TOWER HILL PREFERRED INS CO**
Rating: D
Headquarters: Gainesville, FL
Licensed In: FL
Website: https://www.thig.com
Telephone: (352) 332-8800

Insurer: **TOWER HILL PRIME INS CO**
Rating: D
Headquarters: Gainesville, FL
Licensed In: AL, AZ, AR, FL, GA, IL, IN, KY, MS, MO, NM, NC, SC, TX, WI
Website: https://www.thig.com
Telephone: (352) 332-8800

Insurer: **TOWER HILL SELECT INS CO**
Rating: D
Headquarters: Gainesville, FL
Licensed In: FL
Website: https://www.thig.com
Telephone: (352) 332-8800

Insurer: **UNIVERSAL P&C INS CO**
Rating: D
Headquarters: Fort Lauderdale, FL
Licensed In: AL, DE, FL, GA, HI, IL, IN, IA, MD, MA, MI, MN, NH, NJ, NY, NC, PA, SC, VA, WV
Website: https://universalproperty.com
Telephone: (954) 958-1200

Appendices

Quote Comparison Worksheet

Using the worksheet below is a great way to stay organized as you compare the premium quotes from different insurance companies. It allows you to easily compare companies and how much they will charge you for each type of coverage you may be considering.

If you are planning to contact more than three companies, be sure to make copies of this worksheet beforehand.

Company Name						
Phone # or Web						
Address						
	Limit/Deductible	Price	Limit/Deductible	Price	Limit/Deductible	Price
Personal Property Coverage						
Coverage Type: Actual Cash Value or Replacement Cost						
Liability Coverage						
Additional Living Expenses						
Other						
Discounts						
TOTAL						

Helpful Resources

Contact any of the following organizations for further information about purchasing renters' insurance.

- **Your state department of insurance** - See next page for a specific contact
- **National Association of Insurance Commissioners** - www.naic.org
- **Insurance Information Institute** - www.iii.org
- **Independent Insurance Agents & Brokers of America**
  www.independentagent.com/default.aspx
- **Weiss Ratings, LLC**. - www.weissratings.com

State Insurance Commissioners' Departmental Contact Information

State	Official's Title	Website Address	Telephone
Alabama	Commissioner	www.aldoi.org	(334) 269-3550
Alaska	Director	https://www.commerce.alaska.gov/web/ins/	(800) 467-8725
Arizona	Director	https://insurance.az.gov/	(602) 364-2499
Arkansas	Commissioner	www.insurance.arkansas.gov	(800) 852-5494
California	Commissioner	www.insurance.ca.gov	(800) 927-4357
Colorado	Commissioner	https://www.colorado.gov/pacific/dora/node/90616	(800) 866-7675
Connecticut	Commissioner	http://www.ct.gov/cid/site/default.asp	(800) 203-3447
Delaware	Commissioner	http://delawareinsurance.gov/	(800) 282-8611
Dist. of Columbia	Commissioner	http://disb.dc.gov/	(202) 727-8000
Florida	Commissioner	www.floir.com/	(850) 413-3140
Georgia	Commissioner	www.oci.ga.gov/	(800) 656-2298
Hawaii	Commissioner	http://cca.hawaii.gov/ins/	(808) 586-2790
Idaho	Director	www.doi.idaho.gov	(800) 721-3272
Illinois	Director	www.insurance.illinois.gov/	(866) 445-5364
Indiana	Commissioner	www.in.gov/idoi/	(800) 622-4461
Iowa	Commissioner	https://iid.iowa.gov/	(877) 955-1212
Kansas	Commissioner	www.ksinsurance.org	(800) 432-2484
Kentucky	Commissioner	http://insurance.ky.gov/	(800) 595-6053
Louisiana	Commissioner	www.ldi.la.gov/	(800) 259-5300
Maine	Superintendent	www.maine.gov/pfr/insurance/	(800) 300-5000
Maryland	Commissioner	http://insurance.maryland.gov/Pages/default.aspx	(800) 492-6116
Massachusetts	Commissioner	www.mass.gov/ocabr/government/oca-agencies/doi-lp/	(877) 563-4467
Michigan	Director	http://www.michigan.gov/difs	(877) 999-6442
Minnesota	Commissioner	http://mn.gov/commerce/	(651) 539-1500
Mississippi	Commissioner	http://www.mid.ms.gov/	(601) 359-3569
Missouri	Director	www.insurance.mo.gov	(800) 726-7390
Montana	Commissioner	http://csimt.gov/	(800) 332-6148
Nebraska	Director	www.doi.nebraska.gov/	(402) 471-2201
Nevada	Commissioner	www.doi.nv.gov/	(888) 872-3234
New Hampshire	Commissioner	www.nh.gov/insurance/	(800) 852-3416
New Jersey	Commissioner	www.state.nj.us/dobi/	(800) 446-7467
New Mexico	Superintendent	www.osi.state.nm.us/	(855) 427-5674
New York	Superintendent	www.dfs.ny.gov/	(800) 342-3736
North Carolina	Commissioner	www.ncdoi.com	(855) 408-1212
North Dakota	Commissioner	www.nd.gov/ndins/	(800) 247-0560
Ohio	Lieutenant Governor	www.insurance.ohio.gov	(800) 686-1526
Oklahoma	Commissioner	www.ok.gov/oid/	(800) 522-0071
Oregon Insurance	Commissioner	http://dfr.oregon.gov/Pages/index.aspx	(888) 877-4894
Pennsylvania	Commissioner	www.insurance.pa.gov/	(877) 881-6388
Puerto Rico	Commissioner	www.ocs.gobierno.pr	(787) 304-8686
Rhode Island	Superintendent	www.dbr.state.ri.us/divisions/insurance/	(401) 462-9500
South Carolina	Director	www.doi.sc.gov	(803) 737-6160
South Dakota	Director	http://dlr.sd.gov/insurance/default.aspx	(605) 773-3563
Tennessee	Commissioner	http://tn.gov/commerce/	(615) 741-2241
Texas	Commissioner	www.tdi.texas.gov/	(800) 578-4677
Utah	Commissioner	www.insurance.utah.gov	(800) 439-3805
Vermont	Commissioner	www.dfr.vermont.gov/	(802) 828-3301
Virgin Islands	Lieutenant Governor	http://ltg.gov.vi/division-of-banking-and-insurance.html	(340) 774-7166
Virginia	Commissioner	www.scc.virginia.gov/boi/	(804) 371-9741
Washington	Commissioner	www.insurance.wa.gov	(800) 562-6900
West Virginia	Commissioner	www.wvinsurance.gov	(888) 879-9842
Wisconsin	Commissioner	oci.wi.gov	(800) 236-8517
Wyoming	Commissioner	http://doi.wyo.gov/	(800) 438-5768

2019 Median Rent Estimates for a One-Bedroom Apartment

Data is arranged by State and Area. Monthly rent estimates are the 50th percentile (median) price of a one-bedroom apartment.

Alabama

Area	Rent
Anniston-Oxford-Jacksonville, AL	$545
Auburn-Opelika, AL	$674
Barbour County, AL	$541
Birmingham-Hoover, AL	$824
Bullock County, AL	$548
Butler County, AL	$514
Chambers County, AL	$640
Cherokee County, AL	$524
Chilton County, AL	$597
Choctaw County, AL	$545
Clarke County, AL	$538
Clay County, AL	$549
Cleburne County, AL	$519
Coffee County, AL	$610
Columbus, GA-AL	$771
Conecuh County, AL	$478
Coosa County, AL	$550
Covington County, AL	$491
Crenshaw County, AL	$475
Cullman County, AL	$577
Dale County, AL	$532
Dallas County, AL	$562
Daphne-Fairhope-Foley, AL	$835
Decatur, AL	$557
DeKalb County, AL	$475
Dothan, AL	$557
Escambia County, AL	$555
Fayette County, AL	$549
Florence-Muscle Shoals, AL	$568
Franklin County, AL	$548
Gadsden, AL	$542
Greene County, AL	$549
Henry County, AL	$561

Area	Rent
Huntsville, AL	$743
Jackson County, AL	$605
Lamar County, AL	$546
Macon County, AL	$505
Marengo County, AL	$539
Marion County, AL	$475
Marshall County, AL	$510
Mobile, AL	$730
Monroe County, AL	$549
Montgomery, AL	$743
Perry County, AL	$549
Pickens County, AL	$481
Pike County, AL	$610
Randolph County, AL	$573
Sumter County, AL	$584
Talladega County, AL	$538
Tallapoosa County, AL	$566
Tuscaloosa, AL	$750
Walker County, AL	$529
Washington County, AL	$574
Wilcox County, AL	$549
Winston County, AL	$475

Alaska

Area	Rent
Aleutians East Borough, AK	$890
Aleutians West Census Area, AK	$1,371
Anchorage, AK	$1,067
Bethel Census Area, AK	$1,486
Bristol Bay Borough, AK	$1,004
Denali Borough, AK	$1,233
Dillingham Census Area, AK	$1,212
Fairbanks, AK	$1,085
Haines Borough, AK	$799
Hoonah-Angoon Census Area, AK	$838

Area	Rent
Juneau City and Borough, AK	$1,170
Kenai Peninsula Borough, AK	$921
Ketchikan Gateway Borough, AK	$1,071
Kodiak Island Borough, AK	$1,219
Kusilvak Census Area	$864
Lake and Peninsula Borough, AK	$761
Matanuska-Susitna Borough, AK	$852
Nome Census Area, AK	$1,489
North Slope Borough, AK	$1,273
Northwest Arctic Borough, AK	$1,290
Petersburg Census Area, AK	$892
Prince of Wales-Hyder Census Area, AK	$864
Sitka City and Borough, AK	$1,125
Skagway Municipality, AK	$1,244
Southeast Fairbanks Census Area, AK	$1,093
Valdez-Cordova Census Area, AK	$977
Wrangell City and Borough, AK	$785
Yakutat City and Borough, AK	$935
Yukon-Koyukuk Census Area, AK	$722

Arizona

Area	Rent
Apache County, AZ	$625
Flagstaff, AZ	$1,084
Gila County, AZ	$702
Graham County, AZ	$743
Greenlee County, AZ	$578
La Paz County, AZ	$652
Lake Havasu City-Kingman, AZ	$650

Area	Rent
Navajo County, AZ	$666
Phoenix-Mesa-Scottsdale, AZ	$929
Prescott, AZ	$773
Santa Cruz County, AZ	$601
Sierra Vista-Douglas, AZ	$685
Tucson, AZ	$726
Yuma, AZ	$650

Arkansas

Area	Rent
Arkansas County, AR	$531
Ashley County, AR	$546
Baxter County, AR	$569
Boone County, AR	$510
Bradley County, AR	$550
Calhoun County, AR	$609
Carroll County, AR	$534
Chicot County, AR	$568
Clark County, AR	$527
Clay County, AR	$491
Cleburne County, AR	$562
Columbia County, AR	$581
Conway County, AR	$559
Cross County, AR	$556
Dallas County, AR	$491
Desha County, AR	$491
Drew County, AR	$530
Fayetteville-Springdale-Rogers, AR	$623
Fort Smith, AR-OK	$545
Franklin County, AR	$504
Fulton County, AR	$491
Grant County, AR	$673
Greene County, AR	$631
Hempstead County, AR	$511
Hot Spring County, AR	$577
Hot Springs, AR	$625
Howard County, AR	$495
Independence County, AR	$531
Izard County, AR	$491
Jackson County, AR	$510
Johnson County, AR	$535

Area	Rent
Jonesboro, AR	$627
Lafayette County, AR	$540
Lawrence County, AR	$510
Lee County, AR	$491
Little River County, AR	$491
Little Rock-North Little Rock-Conway, AR	$746
Logan County, AR	$534
Marion County, AR	$528
Memphis, TN-MS-AR	$794
Mississippi County, AR	$541
Monroe County, AR	$516
Montgomery County, AR	$491
Nevada County, AR	$578
Newton County, AR	$501
Ouachita County, AR	$526
Phillips County, AR	$491
Pike County, AR	$568
Pine Bluff, AR	$577
Poinsett County, AR	$491
Polk County, AR	$510
Pope County, AR	$556
Prairie County, AR	$491
Randolph County, AR	$494
Scott County, AR	$491
Searcy County, AR	$495
Sevier County, AR	$503
Sharp County, AR	$491
St. Francis County, AR	$491
Stone County, AR	$503
Texarkana, TX-Texarkana, AR	$663
Union County, AR	$597
Van Buren County, AR	$513
White County, AR	$561
Woodruff County, AR	$508
Yell County, AR	$540

California

Area	Rent
Alpine County, CA	$787
Amador County, CA	$853
Bakersfield, CA	$762

Area	Rent
Calaveras County, CA	$860
Chico, CA	$951
Colusa County, CA	$770
Del Norte County, CA	$782
El Centro, CA	$772
Fresno, CA	$818
Glenn County, CA	$681
Hanford-Corcoran, CA	$864
Humboldt County, CA	$816
Inyo County, CA	$824
Lake County, CA	$790
Lassen County, CA	$696
Los Angeles-Long Beach-Glendale, CA	$1,494
Madera, CA	$826
Mariposa County, CA	$792
Mendocino County, CA	$881
Merced, CA	$720
Modesto, CA	$849
Modoc County, CA	$582
Mono County, CA	$1,012
Napa, CA	$1,385
Nevada County, CA	$999
Oakland-Fremont, CA	$1,892
Oxnard-Thousand Oaks-Ventura, CA	$1,462
Plumas County, CA	$792
Redding, CA	$803
Riverside-San Bernardino-Ontario, CA	$1,068
Sacramento--Roseville--Arden-Arcade, CA	$1,040
Salinas, CA	$1,340
San Benito County, CA	$1,429
San Diego-Carlsbad, CA	$1,590
San Francisco, CA	$2,667
San Jose-Sunnyvale-Santa Clara, CA	$2,446
San Luis Obispo-Paso Robles-Arroyo Grande, CA	$1,275
Santa Ana-Anaheim-Irvine, CA	$1,769
Santa Cruz-Watsonville, CA	$1,979
Santa Maria-Santa Barbara, CA	$1,759
Santa Rosa, CA	$1,540

Area	Rent
Sierra County, CA	$1,041
Siskiyou County, CA	$692
Stockton-Lodi, CA	$875
Tehama County, CA	$658
Trinity County, CA	$683
Tuolumne County, CA	$846
Vallejo-Fairfield, CA	$1,267
Visalia-Porterville, CA	$746
Yolo, CA	$1,102
Yuba City, CA	$715

Colorado

Area	Rent
Alamosa County, CO	$694
Archuleta County, CO	$822
Baca County, CO	$604
Bent County, CO	$706
Boulder, CO	$1,354
Chaffee County, CO	$824
Cheyenne County, CO	$541
Colorado Springs, CO	$897
Conejos County, CO	$564
Costilla County, CO	$618
Crowley County, CO	$689
Custer County, CO	$641
Delta County, CO	$737
Denver-Aurora-Lakewood, CO	$1,308
Dolores County, CO	$653
Eagle County, CO	$1,199
Fort Collins, CO	$1,088
Fremont County, CO	$652
Garfield County, CO	$1,005
Grand County, CO	$862
Grand Junction, CO	$678
Greeley, CO	$856
Gunnison County, CO	$845
Hinsdale County, CO	$807
Huerfano County, CO	$654
Jackson County, CO	$790
Kiowa County, CO	$651
Kit Carson County, CO	$609
La Plata County, CO	$985

Area	Rent
Lake County, CO	$860
Las Animas County, CO	$678
Lincoln County, CO	$620
Logan County, CO	$685
Mineral County, CO	$798
Moffat County, CO	$747
Montezuma County, CO	$674
Montrose County, CO	$718
Morgan County, CO	$645
Otero County, CO	$626
Ouray County, CO	$963
Phillips County, CO	$582
Pitkin County, CO	$1,404
Prowers County, CO	$619
Pueblo, CO	$708
Rio Blanco County, CO	$710
Rio Grande County, CO	$611
Routt County, CO	$1,032
Saguache County, CO	$550
San Juan County, CO	$1,087
San Miguel County, CO	$1,230
Sedgwick County, CO	$541
Summit County, CO	$1,182
Teller County, CO	$851
Washington County, CO	$676
Yuma County, CO	$582

Connecticut

Area	Rent
Bridgeport, CT	$1,110
Colchester-Lebanon, CT	$995
Danbury, CT	$1,342
Hartford-West Hartford-East Hartford, CT	$1,028
Litchfield County, CT	$953
Milford-Ansonia-Seymour, CT	$1,190
New Haven-Meriden, CT	$1,243
Norwich-New London, CT	$958
Southern Middlesex County, CT	$1,145
Stamford-Norwalk, CT	$1,660
Waterbury, CT	$943
Windham County, CT	$876

Deleware

Area	Rent
Dover, DE	$933
Philadelphia-Camden-Wilmington, PA-NJ-DE-MD	$1,073
Sussex County, DE	$879

District of Columbia

Area	Rent
Washington-Arlington-Alexandria, DC-VA-MD	$1,583

Florida

Area	Rent
Baker County, FL	$638
Bradford County, FL	$630
Calhoun County, FL	$629
Cape Coral-Fort Myers, FL	$895
Columbia County, FL	$690
Crestview-Fort Walton Beach-Destin, FL	$916
Deltona-Daytona Beach-Ormond Beach, FL	$918
DeSoto County, FL	$589
Dixie County, FL	$641
Fort Lauderdale, FL	$1,209
Franklin County, FL	$725
Gainesville, FL	$824
Glades County, FL	$634
Gulf County, FL	$739
Hamilton County, FL	$606
Hardee County, FL	$646
Hendry County, FL	$720
Holmes County, FL	$544
Homosassa Springs, FL	$672
Jackson County, FL	$627
Jacksonville, FL	$859
Lafayette County, FL	$716
Lakeland-Winter Haven, FL	$755
Levy County, FL	$545
Liberty County, FL	$606

Area	Rent	Area	Rent	Area	Rent
Madison County, FL	$660	Bacon County, GA	$552	Jackson County, GA	$623
Miami-Miami Beach-Kendall, FL	$1,229	Baldwin County, GA	$653	Jeff Davis County, GA	$526
Monroe County, FL	$1,367	Banks County, GA	$620	Jefferson County, GA	$499
Naples-Immokalee-Marco Island, FL	$1,174	Ben Hill County, GA	$537	Jenkins County, GA	$526
North Port-Sarasota-Bradenton, FL	$993	Berrien County, GA	$499	Johnson County, GA	$576
Ocala, FL	$757	Bleckley County, GA	$534	Lamar County, GA	$637
Okeechobee County, FL	$718	Brunswick, GA	$706	Laurens County, GA	$539
Orlando-Kissimmee-Sanford, FL	$1,067	Bulloch County, GA	$616	Lincoln County, GA	$625
Palm Bay-Melbourne-Titusville, FL	$844	Butts County, GA	$703	Long County, GA	$641
Palm Coast, FL	$991	Calhoun County, GA	$503	Lumpkin County, GA	$674
Panama City-Lynn Haven-Panama City Beach, FL	$923	Camden County, GA	$752	Macon County, GA	$499
Pensacola-Ferry Pass-Brent, FL	$845	Candler County, GA	$499	Macon, GA	$754
Port St. Lucie, FL	$934	Charlton County, GA	$549	Meriwether County, GA	$629
Punta Gorda, FL	$803	Chattanooga, TN-GA	$741	Miller County, GA	$608
Putnam County, FL	$674	Chattooga County, GA	$510	Mitchell County, GA	$565
Sebastian-Vero Beach, FL	$847	Clay County, GA	$499	Monroe County, GA	$709
Sebring, FL	$679	Clinch County, GA	$526	Montgomery County, GA	$576
Suwannee County, FL	$606	Coffee County, GA	$562	Morgan County, GA	$821
Tallahassee, FL	$823	Colquitt County, GA	$556	Murray County, GA	$561
Tampa-St. Petersburg-Clearwater, FL	$978	Cook County, GA	$544	Peach County, GA	$629
Taylor County, FL	$606	Crisp County, GA	$526	Pierce County, GA	$576
The Villages, FL	$679	Dalton, GA	$659	Polk County, GA	$591
Union County, FL	$625	Decatur County, GA	$547	Pulaski County, GA	$608
Wakulla County, FL	$816	Dodge County, GA	$522	Putnam County, GA	$709
Walton County, FL	$798	Dooly County, GA	$611	Quitman County, GA	$526
Washington County, FL	$525	Early County, GA	$576	Rabun County, GA	$578
West Palm Beach-Boca Raton, FL	$1,236	Elbert County, GA	$539	Randolph County, GA	$569
		Emanuel County, GA	$531	Rome, GA	$641
		Evans County, GA	$545	Savannah, GA	$930
		Fannin County, GA	$680	Schley County, GA	$499
		Franklin County, GA	$576	Screven County, GA	$499
		Gainesville, GA	$820	Seminole County, GA	$534
		Gilmer County, GA	$627	Stephens County, GA	$502
		Glascock County, GA	$524	Stewart County, GA	$499
		Gordon County, GA	$557	Sumter County, GA	$570
		Grady County, GA	$623	Talbot County, GA	$705
		Greene County, GA	$629	Taliaferro County, GA	$637
		Habersham County, GA	$571	Tattnall County, GA	$576
		Hancock County, GA	$499	Taylor County, GA	$576
		Haralson County, GA	$726	Telfair County, GA	$503
		Hart County, GA	$551	Thomas County, GA	$644
		Hinesville, GA	$838	Tift County, GA	$555
		Irwin County, GA	$526		

Georgia

Area	Rent
Albany, GA	$604
Appling County, GA	$526
Athens-Clarke County, GA	$714
Atkinson County, GA	$499
Atlanta-Sandy Springs-Roswell, GA	$1,031
Augusta-Richmond County, GA-SC	$748

Toombs County, GA	$559	Clearwater County, ID	$590	Clay County, IL	$609
Towns County, GA	$643	Coeur d'Alene, ID	$685	Coles County, IL	$629
Treutlen County, GA	$499	Custer County, ID	$583	Crawford County, IL	$597
Troup County, GA	$662	Elmore County, ID	$600	Cumberland County, IL	$538
Turner County, GA	$526	Fremont County, ID	$569	Danville, IL	$607
Union County, GA	$576	Gem County, ID	$629	Davenport-Moline-Rock Island, IA-IL	$687
Upson County, GA	$629	Gooding County, ID	$542	De Witt County, IL	$567
Valdosta, GA	$575	Idaho County, ID	$552	Decatur, IL	$611
Ware County, GA	$506	Idaho Falls, ID	$587	DeKalb County, IL	$788
Warner Robins, GA	$838	Jerome County, ID	$605	Douglas County, IL	$532
Warren County, GA	$508	Latah County, ID	$597	Edgar County, IL	$534
Washington County, GA	$576	Lemhi County, ID	$609	Edwards County, IL	$609
Wayne County, GA	$499	Lewis County, ID	$579	Effingham County, IL	$553
Webster County, GA	$538	Lewiston, ID-WA	$641	Fayette County, IL	$540
Wheeler County, GA	$526	Lincoln County, ID	$651	Franklin County, IL	$604
White County, GA	$621	Logan, UT-ID	$592	Fulton County, IL	$632
Wilcox County, GA	$576	Madison County, ID	$649	Gallatin County, IL	$609
Wilkes County, GA	$556	Minidoka County, ID	$611	Greene County, IL	$585
Wilkinson County, GA	$530	Oneida County, ID	$574	Grundy County, IL	$887
		Payette County, ID	$591	Hamilton County, IL	$550
		Pocatello, ID	$561	Hancock County, IL	$555
		Power County, ID	$624	Hardin County, IL	$557

Hawaii

Area	Rent
Hawaii County, HI	$1,170
Kahului-Wailuku-Lahaina, HI	$1,447
Kauai County, HI	$1,332
Urban Honolulu, HI	$1,675

Shoshone County, ID	$582
Teton County, ID	$705
Twin Falls County, ID	$594
Valley County, ID	$595
Washington County, ID	$541

Idaho

Area	Rent
Adams County, ID	$529
Bear Lake County, ID	$530
Benewah County, ID	$586
Bingham County, ID	$559
Blaine County, ID	$799
Boise City, ID	$721
Bonner County, ID	$617
Boundary County, ID	$571
Butte County, ID	$594
Camas County, ID	$531
Caribou County, ID	$529
Cassia County, ID	$553
Clark County, ID	$531

Illinois

Area	Rent
Adams County, IL	$611
Bloomington, IL	$695
Bond County, IL	$652
Brown County, IL	$560
Bureau County, IL	$609
Cape Girardeau, MO-IL	$593
Carroll County, IL	$556
Cass County, IL	$589
Champaign-Urbana, IL	$747
Chicago-Joliet-Naperville, IL	$1,140
Christian County, IL	$596
Clark County, IL	$566

Henderson County, IL	$570
Iroquois County, IL	$566
Jackson County, IL	$603
Jasper County, IL	$598
Jefferson County, IL	$578
Jo Daviess County, IL	$609
Johnson County, IL	$556
Kankakee, IL	$723
Kendall County, IL	$1,045
Knox County, IL	$547
La Salle County, IL	$636
Lawrence County, IL	$547
Lee County, IL	$627
Livingston County, IL	$574
Logan County, IL	$564
Macoupin County, IL	$551
Marion County, IL	$539
Mason County, IL	$615
Massac County, IL	$656
McDonough County, IL	$625

Area	Rent
Montgomery County, IL	$557
Morgan County, IL	$581
Moultrie County, IL	$601
Ogle County, IL	$615
Peoria, IL	$668
Perry County, IL	$609
Pike County, IL	$527
Pope County, IL	$527
Pulaski County, IL	$609
Putnam County, IL	$598
Randolph County, IL	$607
Richland County, IL	$527
Rockford, IL	$640
Saline County, IL	$545
Schuyler County, IL	$540
Scott County, IL	$534
Shelby County, IL	$558
Springfield, IL	$694
St. Louis, MO-IL	$763
Stephenson County, IL	$528
Union County, IL	$527
Wabash County, IL	$573
Warren County, IL	$585
Washington County, IL	$595
Wayne County, IL	$527
White County, IL	$529
Whiteside County, IL	$619
Williamson County, IL	$567

Indiana

Area	Rent
Adams County, IN	$582
Anderson, IN	$641
Blackford County, IN	$529
Bloomington, IN	$777
Carroll County, IN	$541
Cass County, IN	$520
Cincinnati, OH-KY-IN	$722
Clinton County, IN	$576
Columbus, IN	$765
Crawford County, IN	$520
Daviess County, IN	$544
Decatur County, IN	$632
DeKalb County, IN	$585
Dubois County, IN	$535
Elkhart-Goshen, IN	$649
Evansville, IN-KY	$659
Fayette County, IN	$560
Fort Wayne, IN	$649
Fountain County, IN	$584
Franklin County, IN	$575
Fulton County, IN	$613
Gary, IN	$794
Gibson County, IN	$613
Grant County, IN	$573
Greene County, IN	$567
Henry County, IN	$578
Huntington County, IN	$588
Indianapolis-Carmel, IN	$799
Jackson County, IN	$655
Jasper County, IN	$661
Jay County, IN	$520
Jefferson County, IN	$591
Jennings County, IN	$592
Knox County, IN	$580
Kokomo, IN	$587
Kosciusko County, IN	$644
Lafayette-West Lafayette, IN	$740
LaGrange County, IN	$566
Lawrence County, IN	$565
Louisville, KY-IN	$733
Marshall County, IN	$573
Martin County, IN	$556
Miami County, IN	$601
Michigan City-La Porte, IN	$636
Montgomery County, IN	$575
Muncie, IN	$593
Noble County, IN	$598
Orange County, IN	$537
Owen County, IN	$630
Parke County, IN	$568
Perry County, IN	$522
Pike County, IN	$528
Pulaski County, IN	$560
Putnam County, IN	$602
Randolph County, IN	$555
Ripley County, IN	$583
Rush County, IN	$544
Scott County, IN	$649
South Bend-Mishawaka, IN	$696
Spencer County, IN	$520
Starke County, IN	$553
Steuben County, IN	$585
Sullivan County, IN	$634
Switzerland County, IN	$577
Terre Haute, IN	$674
Tipton County, IN	$664
Union County, IN	$633
Wabash County, IN	$562
Warren County, IN	$572
Washington County, IN	$560
Wayne County, IN	$546
White County, IN	$568

Iowa

Area	Rent
Adair County, IA	$502
Adams County, IA	$517
Allamakee County, IA	$506
Ames, IA	$803
Appanoose County, IA	$516
Audubon County, IA	$502
Benton County, IA	$549
Boone County, IA	$666
Bremer County, IA	$590
Buchanan County, IA	$540
Buena Vista County, IA	$527
Butler County, IA	$510
Calhoun County, IA	$580
Carroll County, IA	$502
Cass County, IA	$580
Cedar County, IA	$589
Cedar Rapids, IA	$646
Cerro Gordo County, IA	$592
Cherokee County, IA	$541
Chickasaw County, IA	$566

Area	Rent
Clarke County, IA	$594
Clay County, IA	$518
Clayton County, IA	$526
Clinton County, IA	$614
Crawford County, IA	$516
Davis County, IA	$538
Decatur County, IA	$503
Delaware County, IA	$502
Des Moines County, IA	$606
Des Moines-West Des Moines, IA	$786
Dickinson County, IA	$590
Dubuque, IA	$643
Emmet County, IA	$509
Fayette County, IA	$518
Floyd County, IA	$534
Franklin County, IA	$502
Fremont County, IA	$507
Greene County, IA	$523
Hamilton County, IA	$576
Hancock County, IA	$517
Hardin County, IA	$502
Henry County, IA	$596
Howard County, IA	$580
Humboldt County, IA	$519
Ida County, IA	$545
Iowa City, IA	$735
Iowa County, IA	$534
Jackson County, IA	$573
Jasper County, IA	$569
Jefferson County, IA	$590
Jones County, IA	$555
Keokuk County, IA	$514
Kossuth County, IA	$523
Lee County, IA	$576
Louisa County, IA	$553
Lucas County, IA	$623
Lyon County, IA	$505
Mahaska County, IA	$565
Marion County, IA	$592
Marshall County, IA	$610
Mitchell County, IA	$529
Monona County, IA	$502
Monroe County, IA	$542
Montgomery County, IA	$518
Muscatine County, IA	$698
O'Brien County, IA	$502
Omaha-Council Bluffs, NE-IA	$792
Osceola County, IA	$502
Page County, IA	$518
Palo Alto County, IA	$502
Plymouth County, IA	$559
Pocahontas County, IA	$526
Poweshiek County, IA	$582
Ringgold County, IA	$538
Sac County, IA	$524
Shelby County, IA	$545
Sioux City, IA-NE-SD	$668
Sioux County, IA	$540
Tama County, IA	$559
Taylor County, IA	$503
Union County, IA	$523
Van Buren County, IA	$566
Wapello County, IA	$578
Washington County, IA	$590
Waterloo-Cedar Falls, IA	$704
Wayne County, IA	$502
Webster County, IA	$543
Winnebago County, IA	$510
Winneshiek County, IA	$523
Worth County, IA	$542
Wright County, IA	$515

Kansas

Area	Rent
Allen County, KS	$513
Anderson County, KS	$587
Atchison County, KS	$556
Barber County, KS	$556
Barton County, KS	$522
Bourbon County, KS	$527
Brown County, KS	$508
Chase County, KS	$517
Chautauqua County, KS	$576
Cherokee County, KS	$561
Cheyenne County, KS	$641
Clark County, KS	$604
Clay County, KS	$676
Cloud County, KS	$511
Coffey County, KS	$513
Comanche County, KS	$508
Cowley County, KS	$542
Crawford County, KS	$569
Decatur County, KS	$508
Dickinson County, KS	$528
Edwards County, KS	$508
Elk County, KS	$508
Ellis County, KS	$551
Ellsworth County, KS	$513
Finney County, KS	$609
Ford County, KS	$587
Franklin County, KS	$631
Geary County, KS	$778
Gove County, KS	$508
Graham County, KS	$587
Grant County, KS	$508
Gray County, KS	$547
Greeley County, KS	$555
Greenwood County, KS	$564
Hamilton County, KS	$531
Harper County, KS	$534
Haskell County, KS	$668
Hodgeman County, KS	$545
Jewell County, KS	$553
Kansas City, MO-KS	$839
Kearny County, KS	$508
Kingman County, KS	$524
Kiowa County, KS	$587
Labette County, KS	$536
Lane County, KS	$555
Lawrence, KS	$748
Lincoln County, KS	$577
Logan County, KS	$508
Lyon County, KS	$508
Manhattan, KS	$772
Marion County, KS	$508
Marshall County, KS	$508
McPherson County, KS	$594

Area	Rent
Meade County, KS	$513
Mitchell County, KS	$511
Montgomery County, KS	$525
Morris County, KS	$541
Morton County, KS	$508
Nemaha County, KS	$555
Neosho County, KS	$582
Ness County, KS	$587
Norton County, KS	$508
Osborne County, KS	$587
Ottawa County, KS	$538
Pawnee County, KS	$508
Phillips County, KS	$587
Pratt County, KS	$599
Rawlins County, KS	$508
Reno County, KS	$584
Republic County, KS	$554
Rice County, KS	$517
Rooks County, KS	$527
Rush County, KS	$565
Russell County, KS	$532
Saline County, KS	$611
Scott County, KS	$647
Seward County, KS	$655
Sheridan County, KS	$508
Sherman County, KS	$572
Smith County, KS	$567
St. Joseph, MO-KS	$631
Stafford County, KS	$514
Stanton County, KS	$508
Stevens County, KS	$564
Sumner County, KS	$561
Thomas County, KS	$547
Topeka, KS	$630
Trego County, KS	$595
Wallace County, KS	$564
Washington County, KS	$508
Wichita County, KS	$508
Wichita, KS	$632
Wilson County, KS	$510
Woodson County, KS	$516

Kentucky

Area	Rent
Adair County, KY	$467
Allen County, KY	$519
Anderson County, KY	$659
Ballard County, KY	$529
Barren County, KY	$543
Bath County, KY	$504
Bell County, KY	$511
Bowling Green, KY	$646
Boyle County, KY	$574
Breathitt County, KY	$467
Breckinridge County, KY	$467
Butler County, KY	$484
Caldwell County, KY	$536
Calloway County, KY	$577
Carlisle County, KY	$513
Carroll County, KY	$554
Carter County, KY	$491
Casey County, KY	$534
Clarksville, TN-KY	$731
Clay County, KY	$539
Clinton County, KY	$498
Crittenden County, KY	$513
Cumberland County, KY	$515
Elizabethtown, KY	$608
Elliott County, KY	$537
Estill County, KY	$467
Fleming County, KY	$467
Floyd County, KY	$527
Franklin County, KY	$678
Fulton County, KY	$489
Garrard County, KY	$538
Grant County, KY	$661
Graves County, KY	$494
Grayson County, KY	$539
Green County, KY	$469
Harlan County, KY	$502
Harrison County, KY	$507
Hart County, KY	$516
Hickman County, KY	$489
Hopkins County, KY	$523

Area	Rent
Huntington-Ashland, WV-KY-OH	$651
Jackson County, KY	$489
Johnson County, KY	$486
Knott County, KY	$467
Knox County, KY	$523
Laurel County, KY	$568
Lawrence County, KY	$526
Lee County, KY	$483
Leslie County, KY	$489
Letcher County, KY	$543
Lewis County, KY	$517
Lexington-Fayette, KY	$742
Lincoln County, KY	$470
Livingston County, KY	$559
Logan County, KY	$541
Lyon County, KY	$483
Madison County, KY	$546
Magoffin County, KY	$539
Marion County, KY	$573
Marshall County, KY	$642
Martin County, KY	$474
Mason County, KY	$520
McCracken County, KY	$596
McCreary County, KY	$467
Meade County, KY	$599
Menifee County, KY	$494
Mercer County, KY	$512
Metcalfe County, KY	$540
Monroe County, KY	$479
Montgomery County, KY	$551
Morgan County, KY	$540
Muhlenberg County, KY	$504
Nelson County, KY	$553
Nicholas County, KY	$467
Ohio County, KY	$498
Owen County, KY	$503
Owensboro, KY	$604
Owsley County, KY	$489
Perry County, KY	$489
Pike County, KY	$559
Powell County, KY	$523
Pulaski County, KY	$517

Robertson County, KY	$519
Rockcastle County, KY	$467
Rowan County, KY	$619
Russell County, KY	$512
Shelby County, KY	$664
Simpson County, KY	$590
Taylor County, KY	$524
Todd County, KY	$507
Union County, KY	$540
Washington County, KY	$523
Wayne County, KY	$540
Webster County, KY	$518
Whitley County, KY	$550
Wolfe County, KY	$467

Louisiana

Area	Rent
Acadia Parish, LA	$511
Alexandria, LA	$658
Allen Parish, LA	$523
Assumption Parish, LA	$622
Avoyelles Parish, LA	$548
Baton Rouge, LA	$914
Beauregard Parish, LA	$591
Bienville Parish, LA	$560
Caldwell Parish, LA	$560
Catahoula Parish, LA	$485
Claiborne Parish, LA	$534
Concordia Parish, LA	$503
East Carroll Parish, LA	$488
Evangeline Parish, LA	$510
Franklin Parish, LA	$500
Hammond, LA	$676
Houma-Thibodaux, LA	$719
Iberia Parish, LA	$635
Iberville Parish, LA	$698
Jackson Parish, LA	$542
Jefferson Davis Parish, LA	$560
La Salle Parish, LA	$516
Lafayette, LA	$776
Lake Charles, LA	$711
Lincoln Parish, LA	$663

Madison Parish, LA	$485
Monroe, LA	$623
Morehouse Parish, LA	$560
Natchitoches Parish, LA	$585
New Orleans-Metairie, LA	$898
Red River Parish, LA	$630
Richland Parish, LA	$501
Sabine Parish, LA	$513
Shreveport-Bossier City, LA	$786
St. James Parish, LA	$721
St. Landry Parish, LA	$544
St. Mary Parish, LA	$668
Tensas Parish, LA	$503
Vermilion Parish, LA	$622
Vernon Parish, LA	$807
Washington Parish, LA	$621
Webster Parish, LA	$606
West Carroll Parish, LA	$485
Winn Parish, LA	$520

Maine

Area	Rent
Aroostook County, ME	$661
Bangor, ME	$818
Cumberland County, ME (part)	$868
Franklin County, ME	$695
Hancock County, ME	$837
Kennebec County, ME	$722
Knox County, ME	$826
Lewiston-Auburn, ME	$740
Lincoln County, ME	$833
Oxford County, ME	$729
Penobscot County, ME (part)	$706
Piscataquis County, ME	$666
Portland, ME	$1,126
Sagadahoc County, ME	$876
Somerset County, ME	$704
Waldo County, ME	$810
Washington County, ME	$665
York County, ME (part)	$926
York-Kittery-South	$1,110

Berwick, ME	

Maryland

Area	Rent
Baltimore-Columbia-Towson, MD	$1,159
California-Lexington Park, MD	$1,170
Caroline County, MD	$784
Cumberland, MD-WV	$615
Dorchester County, MD	$847
Garrett County, MD	$611
Hagerstown, MD	$802
Kent County, MD	$856
Salisbury, MD	$964
Somerset County, MD	$821
Talbot County, MD	$953
Worcester County, MD	$891

Massashusetts

Area	Rent
Barnstable Town, MA	$1,237
Berkshire County, MA (part)	$1,014
Boston-Cambridge-Quincy, MA-NH	$1,904
Brockton, MA	$1,215
Dukes County, MA	$1,641
Eastern Worcester County, MA	$1,012
Easton-Raynham, MA	$1,181
Fitchburg-Leominster, MA	$881
Franklin County, MA	$929
Lawrence, MA-NH	$1,123
Lowell, MA	$1,264
Nantucket County, MA	$1,426
New Bedford, MA	$826
Pittsfield, MA	$885
Providence-Fall River, RI-MA	$948
Springfield, MA	$874
Taunton-Mansfield-Norton, MA	$1,024
Western Worcester County, MA	$773
Worcester, MA	$1,021

Michigan

Area	Rent
Alcona County, MI	$587
Alger County, MI	$530
Allegan County, MI	$693
Alpena County, MI	$574
Ann Arbor, MI	$1,004
Antrim County, MI	$610
Arenac County, MI	$561
Baraga County, MI	$529
Barry County, MI	$727
Battle Creek, MI	$633
Bay City, MI	$630
Benzie County, MI	$640
Branch County, MI	$608
Cass County, MI	$612
Charlevoix County, MI	$621
Cheboygan County, MI	$574
Chippewa County, MI	$589
Clare County, MI	$530
Crawford County, MI	$593
Delta County, MI	$567
Detroit-Warren-Livonia, MI	$806
Dickinson County, MI	$598
Emmet County, MI	$669
Flint, MI	$607
Gladwin County, MI	$570
Gogebic County, MI	$579
Grand Rapids-Wyoming, MI	$780
Grand Traverse County, MI	$801
Gratiot County, MI	$531
Hillsdale County, MI	$570
Holland-Grand Haven, MI	$802
Houghton County, MI	$561
Huron County, MI	$560
Ionia County, MI	$618
Iosco County, MI	$611
Iron County, MI	$547
Isabella County, MI	$628
Jackson, MI	$701
Kalamazoo-Portage, MI	$688

Area	Rent
Kalkaska County, MI	$581
Keweenaw County, MI	$529
Lake County, MI	$543
Lansing-East Lansing, MI	$778
Leelanau County, MI	$733
Lenawee County, MI	$626
Livingston County, MI	$813
Luce County, MI	$571
Mackinac County, MI	$611
Manistee County, MI	$562
Marquette County, MI	$604
Mason County, MI	$593
Mecosta County, MI	$598
Menominee County, MI	$605
Midland, MI	$661
Missaukee County, MI	$650
Monroe, MI	$706
Montcalm County, MI	$654
Montmorency County, MI	$544
Muskegon, MI	$645
Newaygo County, MI	$569
Niles-Benton Harbor, MI	$591
Oceana County, MI	$529
Ogemaw County, MI	$614
Ontonagon County, MI	$606
Osceola County, MI	$570
Oscoda County, MI	$584
Otsego County, MI	$624
Presque Isle County, MI	$611
Roscommon County, MI	$590
Saginaw, MI	$670
Sanilac County, MI	$543
Schoolcraft County, MI	$529
Shiawassee County, MI	$569
St. Joseph County, MI	$569
Tuscola County, MI	$565
Wexford County, MI	$624

Minnesota

Area	Rent
Aitkin County, MN	$615
Becker County, MN	$623
Beltrami County, MN	$624
Big Stone County, MN	$564
Brown County, MN	$568
Cass County, MN	$600
Chippewa County, MN	$599
Clearwater County, MN	$577
Cook County, MN	$694
Cottonwood County, MN	$532
Crow Wing County, MN	$655
Douglas County, MN	$641
Duluth, MN-WI	$717
Fargo, ND-MN	$723
Faribault County, MN	$529
Fillmore County, MN	$541
Freeborn County, MN	$539
Goodhue County, MN	$677
Grand Forks, ND-MN	$669
Grant County, MN	$611
Hubbard County, MN	$573
Itasca County, MN	$618
Jackson County, MN	$558
Kanabec County, MN	$667
Kandiyohi County, MN	$603
Kittson County, MN	$529
Koochiching County, MN	$555
La Crosse-Onalaska, WI-MN	$665
Lac qui Parle County, MN	$558
Lake County, MN	$643
Lake of the Woods County, MN	$599
Le Sueur County, MN	$650
Lincoln County, MN	$566
Lyon County, MN	$542
Mahnomen County, MN	$649
Mankato-North Mankato, MN	$753
Marshall County, MN	$548
Martin County, MN	$530
McLeod County, MN	$629
Meeker County, MN	$628
Mille Lacs County, MN	$708
Minneapolis-St. Paul-Bloomington, MN-WI	$986

Area	Rent	Area	Rent	Area	Rent
Morrison County, MN	$558	Chickasaw County, MS	$497	Pike County, MS	$567
Mower County, MN	$602	Choctaw County, MS	$525	Pontotoc County, MS	$533
Murray County, MN	$568	Claiborne County, MS	$561	Prentiss County, MS	$538
Nobles County, MN	$581	Clarke County, MS	$550	Quitman County, MS	$495
Norman County, MN	$546	Clay County, MS	$518	Scott County, MS	$539
Otter Tail County, MN	$577	Coahoma County, MS	$519	Sharkey County, MS	$518
Pennington County, MN	$586	Covington County, MS	$558	Simpson County, MS	$649
Pine County, MN	$635	Franklin County, MS	$518	Smith County, MS	$520
Pipestone County, MN	$607	George County, MS	$621	Stone County, MS	$549
Pope County, MN	$586	Greene County, MS	$596	Sunflower County, MS	$609
Red Lake County, MN	$611	Grenada County, MS	$492	Tallahatchie County, MS	$492
Redwood County, MN	$604	Gulfport-Biloxi, MS	$714	Tate County, MS	$664
Renville County, MN	$559	Hattiesburg, MS	$665	Tippah County, MS	$496
Rice County, MN	$723	Holmes County, MS	$492	Tishomingo County, MS	$569
Rochester, MN	$783	Humphreys County, MS	$569	Tunica County, MS	$701
Rock County, MN	$559	Issaquena County, MS	$518	Union County, MS	$608
Roseau County, MN	$572	Itawamba County, MS	$567	Walthall County, MS	$542
Sibley County, MN	$613	Jackson, MS	$788	Warren County, MS	$605
St. Cloud, MN	$743	Jasper County, MS	$582	Washington County, MS	$577
Steele County, MN	$630	Jefferson County, MS	$518	Wayne County, MS	$518
Stevens County, MN	$617	Jefferson Davis County, MS	$631	Webster County, MS	$569
Swift County, MN	$548	Jones County, MS	$604	Wilkinson County, MS	$518
Todd County, MN	$556	Kemper County, MS	$511	Winston County, MS	$502
Traverse County, MN	$529	Lafayette County, MS	$814	Yalobusha County, MS	$526
Wabasha County, MN	$667	Lauderdale County, MS	$607	Yazoo County, MS	$553
Wadena County, MN	$548	Lawrence County, MS	$612		
Waseca County, MN	$537	Leake County, MS	$519		
Watonwan County, MN	$611	Lee County, MS	$583		

Missouri

Area	Rent
Adair County, MO	$519
Atchison County, MO	$500
Audrain County, MO	$532
Barry County, MO	$495
Barton County, MO	$564
Bates County, MO	$552
Benton County, MO	$513
Butler County, MO	$553
Callaway County, MO	$554
Camden County, MO	$580
Carroll County, MO	$488
Carter County, MO	$510
Cedar County, MO	$509
Chariton County, MO	$493

Wilkin County, MN $529
Winona County, MN $616
Yellow Medicine County, MN $576
Leflore County, MS $507
Lincoln County, MS $536
Lowndes County, MS $614
Marion County, MS $584
Marshall County, MS $635
Monroe County, MS $540
Montgomery County, MS $518
Neshoba County, MS $541
Newton County, MS $538
Noxubee County, MS $516
Oktibbeha County, MS $711
Panola County, MS $552
Pascagoula, MS $709
Pearl River County, MS $626

Mississippi

Area	Rent
Adams County, MS	$571
Alcorn County, MS	$539
Amite County, MS	$526
Attala County, MS	$541
Benton County, MS	$569
Bolivar County, MS	$593
Calhoun County, MS	$544
Carroll County, MS	$492

Clark County, MO	$500	Nodaway County, MO	$540	Broadwater County, MT	$635
Columbia, MO	$696	Oregon County, MO	$488	Carter County, MT	$545
Cooper County, MO	$523	Ozark County, MO	$496	Chouteau County, MT	$541
Crawford County, MO	$560	Pemiscot County, MO	$488	Custer County, MT	$547
Dade County, MO	$533	Perry County, MO	$544	Daniels County, MT	$657
Dallas County, MO	$503	Pettis County, MO	$607	Dawson County, MT	$658
Daviess County, MO	$540	Phelps County, MO	$577	Deer Lodge County, MT	$597
Dent County, MO	$488	Pike County, MO	$601	Fallon County, MT	$595
Douglas County, MO	$488	Polk County, MO	$539	Fergus County, MT	$608
Dunklin County, MO	$496	Pulaski County, MO	$726	Flathead County, MT	$691
Gasconade County, MO	$507	Putnam County, MO	$514	Gallatin County, MT	$731
Gentry County, MO	$492	Ralls County, MO	$589	Garfield County, MT	$545
Grundy County, MO	$513	Randolph County, MO	$579	Glacier County, MT	$546
Harrison County, MO	$538	Reynolds County, MO	$488	Golden Valley County, MT	$554
Henry County, MO	$573	Ripley County, MO	$523	Granite County, MT	$567
Hickory County, MO	$488	Saline County, MO	$536	Great Falls, MT	$618
Holt County, MO	$488	Schuyler County, MO	$500	Hill County, MT	$586
Howard County, MO	$573	Scotland County, MO	$529	Jefferson County, MT	$696
Howell County, MO	$516	Scott County, MO	$546	Judith Basin County, MT	$545
Iron County, MO	$538	Shannon County, MO	$494	Lake County, MT	$643
Jefferson City, MO	$529	Shelby County, MO	$490	Lewis and Clark County, MT	$743
Johnson County, MO	$581	Springfield, MO	$595	Liberty County, MT	$545
Joplin, MO	$601	St. Clair County, MO	$507	Lincoln County, MT	$585
Knox County, MO	$488	St. Francois County, MO	$521	Madison County, MT	$712
Laclede County, MO	$494	Ste. Genevieve County, MO	$567	McCone County, MT	$545
Lawrence County, MO	$534	Stoddard County, MO	$513	Meagher County, MT	$564
Lewis County, MO	$497	Stone County, MO	$608	Mineral County, MT	$545
Linn County, MO	$490	Sullivan County, MO	$561	Missoula, MT	$776
Livingston County, MO	$541	Taney County, MO	$628	Musselshell County, MT	$662
Macon County, MO	$504	Texas County, MO	$488	Park County, MT	$709
Madison County, MO	$527	Vernon County, MO	$541	Petroleum County, MT	$657
Maries County, MO	$515	Washington County, MO	$488	Phillips County, MT	$545
Marion County, MO	$538	Wayne County, MO	$504	Pondera County, MT	$608
McDonald County, MO	$569	Worth County, MO	$488	Powder River County, MT	$529
Mercer County, MO	$494	Wright County, MO	$488	Powell County, MT	$549
Miller County, MO	$593			Prairie County, MT	$545
Mississippi County, MO	$556			Ravalli County, MT	$624
Moniteau County, MO	$488	**Montana**		Richland County, MT	$705
Monroe County, MO	$508	Area	Rent	Roosevelt County, MT	$550
Montgomery County, MO	$525	Beaverhead County, MT	$595	Rosebud County, MT	$611
Morgan County, MO	$542	Big Horn County, MT	$629	Sanders County, MT	$573
New Madrid County, MO	$514	Billings, MT	$729		
		Blaine County, MT	$611		

Area	Rent
Sheridan County, MT	$569
Silver Bow County, MT	$630
Stillwater County, MT	$591
Sweet Grass County, MT	$617
Teton County, MT	$579
Toole County, MT	$611
Treasure County, MT	$600
Valley County, MT	$573
Wheatland County, MT	$545
Wibaux County, MT	$635

Nebraska

Area	Rent
Adams County, NE	$641
Antelope County, NE	$611
Arthur County, NE	$699
Banner County, NE	$594
Blaine County, NE	$572
Boone County, NE	$634
Box Butte County, NE	$551
Boyd County, NE	$529
Brown County, NE	$618
Buffalo County, NE	$655
Burt County, NE	$604
Butler County, NE	$583
Cedar County, NE	$531
Chase County, NE	$673
Cherry County, NE	$700
Cheyenne County, NE	$641
Clay County, NE	$618
Colfax County, NE	$660
Cuming County, NE	$579
Custer County, NE	$537
Dawes County, NE	$611
Dawson County, NE	$625
Deuel County, NE	$616
Dodge County, NE	$664
Dundy County, NE	$594
Fillmore County, NE	$611
Franklin County, NE	$549
Frontier County, NE	$578
Furnas County, NE	$529

Area	Rent
Gage County, NE	$593
Garden County, NE	$540
Garfield County, NE	$535
Gosper County, NE	$618
Grant County, NE	$594
Greeley County, NE	$529
Hall County, NE	$602
Hamilton County, NE	$543
Harlan County, NE	$529
Hayes County, NE	$629
Hitchcock County, NE	$531
Holt County, NE	$616
Hooker County, NE	$594
Howard County, NE	$529
Jefferson County, NE	$529
Johnson County, NE	$533
Kearney County, NE	$761
Keith County, NE	$567
Keya Paha County, NE	$594
Kimball County, NE	$598
Knox County, NE	$580
Lincoln County, NE	$596
Lincoln, NE	$671
Logan County, NE	$529
Loup County, NE	$529
Madison County, NE	$616
McPherson County, NE	$594
Merrick County, NE	$572
Morrill County, NE	$680
Nance County, NE	$611
Nemaha County, NE	$613
Nuckolls County, NE	$611
Otoe County, NE	$609
Pawnee County, NE	$529
Perkins County, NE	$547
Phelps County, NE	$611
Pierce County, NE	$616
Platte County, NE	$649
Polk County, NE	$530
Red Willow County, NE	$564
Richardson County, NE	$595
Rock County, NE	$529
Saline County, NE	$672

Area	Rent
Saunders County, NE	$634
Scotts Bluff County, NE	$637
Seward County, NE	$558
Sheridan County, NE	$599
Sherman County, NE	$535
Sioux County, NE	$551
Stanton County, NE	$637
Thayer County, NE	$547
Thomas County, NE	$594
Thurston County, NE	$546
Valley County, NE	$541
Wayne County, NE	$585
Webster County, NE	$539
Wheeler County, NE	$594
York County, NE	$621

Nevada

Area	Rent
Carson City, NV	$709
Churchill County, NV	$731
Douglas County, NV	$840
Elko County, NV	$757
Esmeralda County, NV	$560
Eureka County, NV	$711
Humboldt County, NV	$776
Lander County, NV	$889
Las Vegas-Henderson-Paradise, NV	$841
Lincoln County, NV	$651
Lyon County, NV	$686
Mineral County, NV	$555
Nye County, NV	$691
Pershing County, NV	$573
Reno, NV	$867
White Pine County, NV	$854

New Hampshire

Area	Rent
Belknap County, NH	$856
Carroll County, NH	$880
Cheshire County, NH	$896
Coos County, NH	$729
Grafton County, NH	$884

Area	Rent
Hillsborough County, NH (part)	$1,012
Manchester, NH	$1,029
Merrimack County, NH	$931
Nashua, NH	$1,154
Portsmouth-Rochester, NH	$977
Sullivan County, NH	$805
Western Rockingham County, NH	$1,245

New Jersey

Area	Rent
Atlantic City-Hammonton, NJ	$1,072
Bergen-Passaic, NJ	$1,425
Jersey City, NJ	$1,435
Middlesex-Somerset-Hunterdon, NJ	$1,451
Monmouth-Ocean, NJ	$1,213
Newark, NJ	$1,275
Ocean City, NJ	$1,070
Trenton, NJ	$1,175
Vineland-Bridgeton, NJ	$990
Warren County, NJ	$1,130

New Mexico

Area	Rent
Albuquerque, NM	$763
Catron County, NM	$549
Chaves County, NM	$668
Cibola County, NM	$665
Colfax County, NM	$612
Curry County, NM	$754
De Baca County, NM	$695
Eddy County, NM	$736
Farmington, NM	$711
Grant County, NM	$683
Guadalupe County, NM	$624
Harding County, NM	$549
Hidalgo County, NM	$611
Las Cruces, NM	$603
Lea County, NM	$794
Lincoln County, NM	$754
Los Alamos County, NM	$984
Luna County, NM	$557
McKinley County, NM	$727
Mora County, NM	$684
Otero County, NM	$644
Quay County, NM	$529
Rio Arriba County, NM	$639
Roosevelt County, NM	$670
San Miguel County, NM	$744
Santa Fe, NM	$999
Sierra County, NM	$615
Socorro County, NM	$659
Taos County, NM	$842
Union County, NM	$532

New York

Area	Rent
Albany-Schenectady-Troy, NY	$966
Allegany County, NY	$581
Binghamton, NY	$672
Buffalo-Cheektowaga-Niagara Falls, NY	$738
Cattaraugus County, NY	$587
Cayuga County, NY	$653
Chautauqua County, NY	$591
Chenango County, NY	$621
Clinton County, NY	$687
Columbia County, NY	$790
Cortland County, NY	$701
Delaware County, NY	$623
Elmira, NY	$719
Essex County, NY	$713
Franklin County, NY	$641
Fulton County, NY	$664
Genesee County, NY	$666
Glens Falls, NY	$799
Greene County, NY	$827
Hamilton County, NY	$686
Ithaca, NY	$1,026
Kingston, NY	$1,018
Lewis County, NY	$692
Montgomery County, NY	$678
Nassau-Suffolk, NY	$1,669
New York, NY	$1,744
Otsego County, NY	$688
Poughkeepsie-Newburgh-Middletown, NY	$1,140
Rochester, NY	$806
Schuyler County, NY	$622
Seneca County, NY	$720
St. Lawrence County, NY	$672
Steuben County, NY	$661
Sullivan County, NY	$833
Syracuse, NY	$729
Utica-Rome, NY	$647
Watertown-Fort Drum, NY	$963
Westchester County, NY Statutory Exception Area	$1,587
Wyoming County, NY	$563
Yates County, NY	$687

North Carolina

Area	Rent
Alleghany County, NC	$515
Anson County, NC	$621
Ashe County, NC	$513
Asheville, NC	$875
Avery County, NC	$627
Beaufort County, NC	$585
Bertie County, NC	$604
Bladen County, NC	$540
Brunswick County, NC	$816
Burlington, NC	$684
Camden County, NC	$916
Carteret County, NC	$714
Caswell County, NC	$551
Charlotte-Concord-Gastonia, NC-SC	$963
Cherokee County, NC	$616
Chowan County, NC	$726
Clay County, NC	$651
Cleveland County, NC	$630
Columbus County, NC	$539
Craven County, NC	$717
Dare County, NC	$832
Davidson County, NC	$585

Duplin County, NC	$566
Durham-Chapel Hill, NC	$965
Fayetteville, NC	$810
Gates County, NC	$612
Goldsboro, NC	$617
Graham County, NC	$544
Granville County, NC	$657
Greene County, NC	$537
Greensboro-High Point, NC	$706
Greenville, NC	$653
Halifax County, NC	$631
Harnett County, NC	$642
Haywood County, NC	$785
Hertford County, NC	$589
Hickory-Lenoir-Morganton, NC	$549
Hoke County, NC	$690
Hyde County, NC	$742
Iredell County, NC	$846
Jackson County, NC	$640
Jacksonville, NC	$718
Jones County, NC	$565
Lee County, NC	$677
Lenoir County, NC	$586
Lincoln County, NC	$700
Macon County, NC	$650
Martin County, NC	$522
McDowell County, NC	$582
Mitchell County, NC	$522
Montgomery County, NC	$555
Moore County, NC	$758
Northampton County, NC	$538
Pamlico County, NC	$614
Pasquotank County, NC	$669
Pender County, NC	$735
Perquimans County, NC	$701
Person County, NC	$569
Polk County, NC	$624
Raleigh, NC	$1,015
Richmond County, NC	$576
Robeson County, NC	$519
Rockingham County, NC	$513
Rocky Mount, NC	$596
Rowan County, NC	$719
Rutherford County, NC	$513
Sampson County, NC	$522
Scotland County, NC	$579
Stanly County, NC	$571
Surry County, NC	$526
Swain County, NC	$596
Transylvania County, NC	$628
Tyrrell County, NC	$568
Vance County, NC	$590
Virginia Beach-Norfolk-Newport News, VA-NC	$993
Warren County, NC	$557
Washington County, NC	$559
Watauga County, NC	$783
Wilkes County, NC	$513
Wilmington, NC	$838
Wilson County, NC	$713
Winston-Salem, NC	$624
Yancey County, NC	$551

North Dakota

Area	Rent
Adams County, ND	$611
Barnes County, ND	$600
Benson County, ND	$611
Billings County, ND	$692
Bismarck, ND	$712
Bottineau County, ND	$587
Bowman County, ND	$587
Burke County, ND	$773
Cavalier County, ND	$611
Dickey County, ND	$602
Divide County, ND	$529
Dunn County, ND	$999
Eddy County, ND	$611
Emmons County, ND	$629
Foster County, ND	$578
Golden Valley County, ND	$776
Grant County, ND	$607
Griggs County, ND	$529
Hettinger County, ND	$690
Kidder County, ND	$611
LaMoure County, ND	$576
Logan County, ND	$626
McHenry County, ND	$626
McIntosh County, ND	$611
McKenzie County, ND	$840
McLean County, ND	$664
Mercer County, ND	$646
Mountrail County, ND	$833
Nelson County, ND	$611
Oliver County, ND	$738
Pembina County, ND	$611
Pierce County, ND	$630
Ramsey County, ND	$607
Ransom County, ND	$615
Renville County, ND	$572
Richland County, ND	$543
Rolette County, ND	$611
Sargent County, ND	$581
Sheridan County, ND	$692
Sioux County, ND	$546
Slope County, ND	$692
Stark County, ND	$906
Steele County, ND	$576
Stutsman County, ND	$601
Towner County, ND	$535
Traill County, ND	$598
Walsh County, ND	$611
Ward County, ND	$887
Wells County, ND	$611
Williams County, ND	$807

Ohio

Area	Rent
Adams County, OH	$536
Akron, OH	$667
Ashland County, OH	$561
Ashtabula County, OH	$560
Athens County, OH	$715
Auglaize County, OH	$547
Brown County, OH	$606

Area	Rent	Area	Rent	Area	Rent
Canton-Massillon, OH	$623	Scioto County, OH	$596	Grant County, OK	$615
Champaign County, OH	$565	Seneca County, OH	$530	Greer County, OK	$662
Cleveland-Elyria, OH	$723	Shelby County, OH	$607	Harmon County, OK	$545
Clinton County, OH	$581	Springfield, OH	$640	Harper County, OK	$545
Columbiana County, OH	$570	Toledo, OH	$595	Haskell County, OK	$529
Columbus, OH	$815	Tuscarawas County, OH	$589	Hughes County, OK	$532
Coshocton County, OH	$527	Union County, OH	$754	Jackson County, OK	$607
Crawford County, OH	$551	Van Wert County, OH	$522	Jefferson County, OK	$529
Darke County, OH	$523	Vinton County, OH	$596	Johnston County, OK	$556
Dayton, OH	$636	Washington County, OH	$561	Kay County, OK	$552
Defiance County, OH	$554	Wayne County, OH	$609	Kingfisher County, OK	$646
Erie County, OH	$606	Weirton-Steubenville, WV-OH	$586	Kiowa County, OK	$529
Fayette County, OH	$595	Wheeling, WV-OH	$594	Latimer County, OK	$584
Gallia County, OH	$596	Williams County, OH	$556	Lawton, OK	$598
Guernsey County, OH	$560	Wyandot County, OH	$533	Le Flore County, OK	$552
Hancock County, OH	$605	Youngstown-Warren-Boardman, OH	$576	Lincoln County, OK	$529
Hardin County, OH	$525			Love County, OK	$606
Harrison County, OH	$532			Major County, OK	$559
Henry County, OH	$622	**Oklahoma**		Marshall County, OK	$541
Highland County, OH	$592	Area	Rent	Mayes County, OK	$559
Hocking County, OH	$572	Adair County, OK	$530	McCurtain County, OK	$529
Holmes County, OH	$539	Alfalfa County, OK	$556	McIntosh County, OK	$611
Huron County, OH	$550	Atoka County, OK	$529	Murray County, OK	$611
Jackson County, OH	$563	Beaver County, OK	$573	Muskogee County, OK	$562
Knox County, OH	$577	Beckham County, OK	$684	Noble County, OK	$611
Lima, OH	$597	Blaine County, OK	$566	Nowata County, OK	$624
Logan County, OH	$596	Bryan County, OK	$561	Okfuskee County, OK	$561
Mansfield, OH	$541	Caddo County, OK	$542	Oklahoma City, OK	$733
Marion County, OH	$605	Carter County, OK	$649	Okmulgee County, OK	$557
Meigs County, OH	$564	Cherokee County, OK	$587	Ottawa County, OK	$599
Mercer County, OH	$529	Choctaw County, OK	$529	Pawnee County, OK	$564
Monroe County, OH	$594	Cimarron County, OK	$545	Payne County, OK	$688
Morgan County, OH	$596	Coal County, OK	$529	Pittsburg County, OK	$596
Muskingum County, OH	$591	Cotton County, OK	$611	Pontotoc County, OK	$576
Noble County, OH	$565	Craig County, OK	$588	Pottawatomie County, OK	$600
Ottawa County, OH	$614	Custer County, OK	$549	Pushmataha County, OK	$529
Paulding County, OH	$566	Delaware County, OK	$568	Roger Mills County, OK	$611
Perry County, OH	$574	Dewey County, OK	$564	Seminole County, OK	$529
Pike County, OH	$573	Ellis County, OK	$601	Stephens County, OK	$578
Preble County, OH	$554	Enid, OK	$613	Texas County, OK	$672
Putnam County, OH	$601	Garvin County, OK	$585	Tillman County, OK	$545
Ross County, OH	$602	Grady County, OK	$560	Tulsa, OK	$714
Sandusky County, OH	$565				

Area	Rent
Washington County, OK	$649
Washita County, OK	$625
Woods County, OK	$639
Woodward County, OK	$683

Oregon

Area	Rent
Albany, OR	$798
Baker County, OR	$557
Bend-Redmond, OR	$942
Clatsop County, OR	$745
Coos County, OR	$728
Corvallis, OR	$929
Crook County, OR	$612
Curry County, OR	$812
Douglas County, OR	$792
Eugene-Springfield, OR	$823
Gilliam County, OR	$615
Grant County, OR	$598
Grants Pass, OR	$768
Harney County, OR	$588
Hood River County, OR	$952
Jefferson County, OR	$635
Klamath County, OR	$595
Lake County, OR	$574
Lincoln County, OR	$734
Malheur County, OR	$567
Medford, OR	$783
Morrow County, OR	$582
Portland-Vancouver-Hillsboro, OR-WA	$1,301
Salem, OR	$767
Sherman County, OR	$675
Tillamook County, OR	$671
Umatilla County, OR	$605
Union County, OR	$575
Wallowa County, OR	$652
Wasco County, OR	$872
Wheeler County, OR	$542

Pennsylvania

Area	Rent
Allentown-Bethlehem-Easton, PA	$936
Altoona, PA	$684
Armstrong County, PA	$634
Bedford County, PA	$606
Bradford County, PA	$580
Cameron County, PA	$523
Chambersburg-Waynesboro, PA	$748
Clarion County, PA	$602
Clearfield County, PA	$587
Clinton County, PA	$603
Columbia County, PA	$702
Crawford County, PA	$581
East Stroudsburg, PA	$930
Elk County, PA	$533
Erie, PA	$673
Forest County, PA	$578
Fulton County, PA	$604
Gettysburg, PA	$803
Greene County, PA	$635
Harrisburg-Carlisle, PA	$865
Huntingdon County, PA	$563
Indiana County, PA	$685
Jefferson County, PA	$547
Johnstown, PA	$603
Juniata County, PA	$547
Lancaster, PA	$931
Lawrence County, PA	$621
Lebanon, PA	$759
McKean County, PA	$555
Mifflin County, PA	$598
Montour County, PA	$740
Northumberland County, PA	$586
Pike County, PA	$955
Pittsburgh, PA	$781
Potter County, PA	$591
Reading, PA	$846
Schuylkill County, PA	$601
Scranton--Wilkes-Barre, PA	$677
Sharon, PA	$589

Area	Rent
Snyder County, PA	$575
Somerset County, PA	$563
State College, PA	$961
Sullivan County, PA	$570
Susquehanna County, PA	$602
Tioga County, PA	$674
Union County, PA	$649
Venango County, PA	$560
Warren County, PA	$581
Wayne County, PA	$722
Williamsport, PA	$745
York-Hanover, PA	$773

Rhode Island

Area	Rent
Newport-Middleton-Portsmouth, RI	$1,145
Westerly-Hopkinton-New Shoreham, RI	$943

South Carolina

Area	Rent
Abbeville County, SC	$520
Allendale County, SC	$541
Anderson, SC	$648
Bamberg County, SC	$581
Barnwell County, SC	$641
Beaufort County, SC	$1,065
Charleston-North Charleston, SC	$1,043
Cherokee County, SC	$556
Chester County, SC	$569
Chesterfield County, SC	$601
Clarendon County, SC	$577
Colleton County, SC	$713
Columbia, SC	$903
Darlington County, SC	$641
Dillon County, SC	$592
Florence, SC	$652
Georgetown County, SC	$665
Greenville-Mauldin-Easley, SC	$818
Greenwood County, SC	$619
Hampton County, SC	$520

Area	Rent
Jasper County, SC	$866
Kershaw County, SC	$715
Lancaster County, SC	$646
Laurens County, SC	$610
Lee County, SC	$532
Marion County, SC	$601
Marlboro County, SC	$563
McCormick County, SC	$540
Myrtle Beach-North Myrtle Beach-Conway, SC	$845
Newberry County, SC	$604
Oconee County, SC	$555
Orangeburg County, SC	$574
Spartanburg, SC	$667
Sumter, SC	$681
Union County, SC	$522
Williamsburg County, SC	$528

South Dakota

Area	Rent
Aurora County, SD	$538
Beadle County, SD	$586
Bennett County, SD	$611
Bon Homme County, SD	$563
Brookings County, SD	$658
Brown County, SD	$592
Brule County, SD	$568
Buffalo County, SD	$581
Butte County, SD	$584
Campbell County, SD	$529
Charles Mix County, SD	$537
Clark County, SD	$637
Clay County, SD	$624
Codington County, SD	$590
Corson County, SD	$594
Custer County, SD	$720
Davison County, SD	$643
Day County, SD	$610
Deuel County, SD	$611
Dewey County, SD	$596
Douglas County, SD	$598
Edmunds County, SD	$610

Area	Rent
Fall River County, SD	$654
Faulk County, SD	$544
Grant County, SD	$568
Gregory County, SD	$561
Haakon County, SD	$636
Hamlin County, SD	$575
Hand County, SD	$542
Hanson County, SD	$529
Harding County, SD	$557
Hughes County, SD	$584
Hutchinson County, SD	$562
Hyde County, SD	$529
Jackson County, SD	$529
Jerauld County, SD	$611
Jones County, SD	$529
Kingsbury County, SD	$529
Lake County, SD	$592
Lawrence County, SD	$608
Lyman County, SD	$543
Marshall County, SD	$537
McPherson County, SD	$630
Meade County, SD	$665
Mellette County, SD	$581
Miner County, SD	$529
Moody County, SD	$584
Oglala Lakota County	$529
Perkins County, SD	$566
Potter County, SD	$658
Rapid City, SD	$711
Roberts County, SD	$537
Sanborn County, SD	$611
Sioux Falls, SD	$765
Spink County, SD	$563
Stanley County, SD	$634
Sully County, SD	$529
Todd County, SD	$529
Tripp County, SD	$529
Walworth County, SD	$611
Yankton County, SD	$582
Ziebach County, SD	$529

Tennessee

Area	Rent
Bedford County, TN	$586
Benton County, TN	$530
Bledsoe County, TN	$542
Campbell County, TN	$505
Carroll County, TN	$535
Claiborne County, TN	$487
Clay County, TN	$481
Cleveland, TN	$635
Cocke County, TN	$478
Coffee County, TN	$542
Crockett County, TN	$529
Cumberland County, TN	$517
Decatur County, TN	$541
DeKalb County, TN	$468
Dyer County, TN	$513
Fentress County, TN	$541
Franklin County, TN	$470
Gibson County, TN	$584
Giles County, TN	$566
Grainger County, TN	$594
Greene County, TN	$475
Grundy County, TN	$496
Hancock County, TN	$488
Hardeman County, TN	$469
Hardin County, TN	$569
Haywood County, TN	$516
Henderson County, TN	$524
Henry County, TN	$513
Hickman County, TN	$740
Houston County, TN	$595
Humphreys County, TN	$553
Jackson County, TN	$468
Jackson, TN	$678
Johnson City, TN	$594
Johnson County, TN	$544
Kingsport-Bristol-Bristol, TN-VA	$549
Knoxville, TN	$747
Lake County, TN	$518
Lauderdale County, TN	$547
Lawrence County, TN	$533

Area	Rent
Lewis County, TN	$481
Lincoln County, TN	$516
Macon County, TN	$566
Marshall County, TN	$561
Maury County, TN	$764
McMinn County, TN	$583
McNairy County, TN	$468
Meigs County, TN	$561
Monroe County, TN	$539
Moore County, TN	$481
Morgan County, TN	$559
Morristown, TN	$571
Nashville-Davidson--Murfreesboro--Franklin, TN	$970
Obion County, TN	$508
Overton County, TN	$470
Perry County, TN	$476
Pickett County, TN	$481
Putnam County, TN	$570
Rhea County, TN	$521
Roane County, TN	$623
Scott County, TN	$468
Sevier County, TN	$672
Smith County, TN	$556
Stewart County, TN	$556
Van Buren County, TN	$507
Warren County, TN	$511
Wayne County, TN	$468
Weakley County, TN	$502
White County, TN	$497

Texas

Area	Rent
Abilene, TX	$667
Amarillo, TX	$702
Anderson County, TX	$719
Andrews County, TX	$825
Angelina County, TX	$743
Aransas County, TX	$847
Atascosa County, TX	$692
Austin County, TX	$874
Austin-Round Rock, TX	$1,170
Bailey County, TX	$611
Baylor County, TX	$535
Beaumont-Port Arthur, TX	$788
Bee County, TX	$735
Blanco County, TX	$674
Borden County, TX	$644
Bosque County, TX	$585
Brazoria County, TX	$1,015
Brewster County, TX	$634
Briscoe County, TX	$557
Brooks County, TX	$557
Brown County, TX	$630
Brownsville-Harlingen, TX	$603
Burnet County, TX	$764
Calhoun County, TX	$736
Camp County, TX	$652
Cass County, TX	$529
Castro County, TX	$616
Cherokee County, TX	$575
Childress County, TX	$638
Cochran County, TX	$536
Coke County, TX	$529
Coleman County, TX	$529
College Station-Bryan, TX	$811
Collingsworth County, TX	$563
Colorado County, TX	$533
Comanche County, TX	$610
Concho County, TX	$631
Cooke County, TX	$705
Corpus Christi, TX	$940
Cottle County, TX	$716
Crane County, TX	$557
Crockett County, TX	$557
Culberson County, TX	$704
Dallam County, TX	$735
Dallas, TX	$1,070
Dawson County, TX	$611
Deaf Smith County, TX	$638
Delta County, TX	$533
DeWitt County, TX	$606
Dickens County, TX	$611
Dimmit County, TX	$644
Donley County, TX	$548
Duval County, TX	$611
Eastland County, TX	$529
Edwards County, TX	$644
El Paso, TX	$732
Erath County, TX	$706
Falls County, TX	$538
Fannin County, TX	$627
Fayette County, TX	$637
Fisher County, TX	$557
Floyd County, TX	$657
Foard County, TX	$644
Fort Worth-Arlington, TX	$911
Franklin County, TX	$585
Freestone County, TX	$577
Frio County, TX	$642
Gaines County, TX	$557
Garza County, TX	$583
Gillespie County, TX	$774
Glasscock County, TX	$644
Gonzales County, TX	$580
Gray County, TX	$617
Grimes County, TX	$599
Hale County, TX	$602
Hall County, TX	$568
Hamilton County, TX	$612
Hansford County, TX	$606
Hardeman County, TX	$561
Harrison County, TX	$726
Hartley County, TX	$721
Haskell County, TX	$611
Hemphill County, TX	$648
Henderson County, TX	$695
Hill County, TX	$618
Hockley County, TX	$634
Hood County, TX	$890
Hopkins County, TX	$628
Houston County, TX	$567
Houston-The Woodlands-Sugar Land, TX	$976
Howard County, TX	$772

County	Rate	County	Rate	County	Rate
Hudspeth County, TX	$713	McCulloch County, TX	$597	Scurry County, TX	$699
Hutchinson County, TX	$637	McMullen County, TX	$644	Shackelford County, TX	$601
Jack County, TX	$696	Medina County, TX	$651	Shelby County, TX	$529
Jackson County, TX	$684	Menard County, TX	$598	Sherman County, TX	$611
Jasper County, TX	$627	Midland, TX	$1,189	Sherman-Denison, TX	$744
Jeff Davis County, TX	$874	Milam County, TX	$566	Somervell County, TX	$726
Jim Hogg County, TX	$586	Mills County, TX	$596	Starr County, TX	$546
Jim Wells County, TX	$677	Mitchell County, TX	$546	Stephens County, TX	$540
Karnes County, TX	$624	Montague County, TX	$685	Sterling County, TX	$644
Kendall County, TX	$1,027	Moore County, TX	$666	Stonewall County, TX	$644
Kenedy County, TX	$644	Morris County, TX	$559	Sutton County, TX	$630
Kent County, TX	$557	Motley County, TX	$557	Swisher County, TX	$538
Kerr County, TX	$793	Nacogdoches County, TX	$737	Terrell County, TX	$677
Killeen-Temple, TX	$626	Navarro County, TX	$668	Terry County, TX	$569
Kimble County, TX	$679	Newton County, TX	$568	Throckmorton County, TX	$557
King County, TX	$820	Nolan County, TX	$556	Titus County, TX	$609
Kinney County, TX	$665	Ochiltree County, TX	$623	Trinity County, TX	$651
Kleberg County, TX	$670	Odessa, TX	$991	Tyler County, TX	$649
Knox County, TX	$557	Oldham County, TX	$752	Tyler, TX	$789
La Salle County, TX	$584	Palo Pinto County, TX	$626	Upton County, TX	$611
Lamar County, TX	$634	Panola County, TX	$588	Uvalde County, TX	$656
Lamb County, TX	$622	Parmer County, TX	$611	Val Verde County, TX	$591
Lampasas County, TX	$575	Pecos County, TX	$688	Van Zandt County, TX	$627
Laredo, TX	$712	Polk County, TX	$590	Victoria, TX	$830
Lavaca County, TX	$576	Presidio County, TX	$557	Waco, TX	$668
Lee County, TX	$682	Rains County, TX	$608	Walker County, TX	$820
Leon County, TX	$562	Reagan County, TX	$708	Ward County, TX	$673
Limestone County, TX	$637	Real County, TX	$681	Washington County, TX	$812
Lipscomb County, TX	$645	Red River County, TX	$547	Wharton County, TX	$677
Live Oak County, TX	$535	Reeves County, TX	$617	Wheeler County, TX	$640
Llano County, TX	$653	Refugio County, TX	$723	Wichita Falls, TX	$629
Longview, TX	$813	Roberts County, TX	$644	Wilbarger County, TX	$615
Loving County, TX	$644	Runnels County, TX	$559	Willacy County, TX	$557
Lubbock, TX	$764	Rusk County, TX	$635	Winkler County, TX	$557
Lynn County, TX	$669	Sabine County, TX	$574	Wise County, TX	$924
Madison County, TX	$680	San Angelo, TX	$788	Wood County, TX	$626
Marion County, TX	$577	San Antonio-New Braunfels, TX	$905	Yoakum County, TX	$622
Martin County, TX	$560	San Augustine County, TX	$566	Young County, TX	$564
Mason County, TX	$838			Zapata County, TX	$611
Matagorda County, TX	$689	San Jacinto County, TX	$606	Zavala County, TX	$611
Maverick County, TX	$594	San Saba County, TX	$529		
McAllen-Edinburg-Mission, TX	$618	Schleicher County, TX	$580		

Utah

Area	Rent
Beaver County, UT	$545
Box Elder County, UT	$575
Carbon County, UT	$561
Daggett County, UT	$661
Duchesne County, UT	$713
Emery County, UT	$611
Garfield County, UT	$545
Grand County, UT	$686
Iron County, UT	$622
Kane County, UT	$769
Millard County, UT	$528
Ogden-Clearfield, UT	$755
Piute County, UT	$608
Provo-Orem, UT	$786
Rich County, UT	$555
Salt Lake City, UT	$923
San Juan County, UT	$611
Sanpete County, UT	$578
Sevier County, UT	$598
St. George, UT	$740
Summit County, UT	$1,095
Tooele County, UT	$796
Uintah County, UT	$772
Wasatch County, UT	$823
Wayne County, UT	$611

Vermont

Area	Rent
Addison County, VT	$942
Bennington County, VT	$882
Burlington-South Burlington, VT	$1,279
Caledonia County, VT	$758
Essex County, VT	$613
Lamoille County, VT	$867
Orange County, VT	$777
Orleans County, VT	$703
Rutland County, VT	$825
Washington County, VT	$842
Windham County, VT	$835
Windsor County, VT	$860

Virginia

Area	Rent
Accomack County, VA	$682
Alleghany County-Clifton Forge city-Covington city, VA	$566
Bath County, VA	$619
Blacksburg-Christiansburg-Radford, VA	$805
Bland County, VA	$578
Brunswick County, VA	$689
Buchanan County, VA	$646
Buckingham County, VA	$732
Carroll County-Galax city, VA	$611
Charlotte County, VA	$563
Charlottesville, VA	$1,237
Culpeper County, VA	$850
Cumberland County, VA	$820
Dickenson County, VA	$611
Essex County, VA	$743
Floyd County, VA	$611
Franklin County, VA	$559
Giles County, VA	$529
Grayson County, VA	$611
Greensville County-Emporia city, VA	$637
Halifax County, VA	$533
Harrisonburg, VA	$716
Henry County-Martinsville city, VA	$538
Highland County, VA	$563
King and Queen County, VA	$808
King George County, VA	$961
Lancaster County, VA	$836
Lee County, VA	$611
Louisa County, VA	$908
Lunenburg County, VA	$654
Lynchburg, VA	$676
Madison County, VA	$803
Mecklenburg County, VA	$619
Middlesex County, VA	$815
Northampton County, VA	$739
Northumberland County, VA	$619
Nottoway County, VA	$746
Orange County, VA	$806
Page County, VA	$659
Patrick County, VA	$611
Pittsylvania County-Danville city, VA	$554
Prince Edward County, VA	$708
Pulaski County, VA	$611
Rappahannock County, VA	$868
Richmond County, VA	$682
Richmond, VA	$996
Roanoke, VA	$685
Rockbridge County-Buena Vista city-Lexington city, VA	$704
Russell County, VA	$581
Shenandoah County, VA	$650
Smyth County, VA	$553
Southampton County-Franklin city, VA	$751
Staunton-Waynesboro, VA	$692
Surry County, VA	$720
Tazewell County, VA	$589
Warren County, VA	$807
Westmoreland County, VA	$751
Winchester, VA-WV	$779
Wise County-Norton city, VA	$569
Wythe County, VA	$563

Washington

Area	Rent
Adams County, WA	$699
Bellingham, WA	$849
Bremerton-Silverdale, WA	$993
Clallam County, WA	$785
Columbia County, WA	$727
Ferry County, WA	$627
Garfield County, WA	$645
Grant County, WA	$693

Area	Rent
Grays Harbor County, WA	$683
Island County, WA	$965
Jefferson County, WA	$812
Kennewick-Richland, WA	$818
Kittitas County, WA	$762
Klickitat County, WA	$726
Lewis County, WA	$738
Lincoln County, WA	$556
Longview, WA	$755
Mason County, WA	$824
Mount Vernon-Anacortes, WA	$819
Okanogan County, WA	$680
Olympia-Tumwater, WA	$1,003
Pacific County, WA	$715
Pend Oreille County, WA	$627
San Juan County, WA	$1,009
Seattle-Bellevue, WA	$1,664
Spokane, WA	$669
Stevens County, WA	$604
Tacoma, WA	$1,036
Wahkiakum County, WA	$597
Walla Walla County, WA	$767
Wenatchee, WA	$777
Whitman County, WA	$716
Yakima, WA	$669

West Virginia

Area	Rent
Barbour County, WV	$503
Boone County, WV	$528
Braxton County, WV	$545
Calhoun County, WV	$516
Charleston, WV	$705
Doddridge County, WV	$507
Fayette County, WV	$544
Gilmer County, WV	$522
Grant County, WV	$572
Greenbrier County, WV	$666
Hardy County, WV	$504
Harrison County, WV	$624
Jackson County, WV	$561

Area	Rent
Jefferson County, WV	$821
Lewis County, WV	$581
Lincoln County, WV	$541
Logan County, WV	$507
Marion County, WV	$624
Martinsburg, WV	$882
Mason County, WV	$540
McDowell County, WV	$545
Mercer County, WV	$526
Mingo County, WV	$543
Monroe County, WV	$520
Morgan County, WV	$666
Morgantown, WV	$725
Nicholas County, WV	$533
Parkersburg-Vienna, WV	$644
Pendleton County, WV	$502
Pleasants County, WV	$579
Pocahontas County, WV	$507
Putnam County, WV	$679
Raleigh County, WV	$694
Randolph County, WV	$583
Ritchie County, WV	$560
Roane County, WV	$523
Summers County, WV	$502
Taylor County, WV	$598
Tucker County, WV	$563
Tyler County, WV	$570
Upshur County, WV	$555
Webster County, WV	$534
Wetzel County, WV	$513
Wyoming County, WV	$516

Wisconsin

Area	Rent
Adams County, WI	$567
Appleton, WI	$642
Ashland County, WI	$559
Barron County, WI	$580
Bayfield County, WI	$599
Buffalo County, WI	$576
Burnett County, WI	$564
Clark County, WI	$553

Area	Rent
Columbia County, WI	$693
Crawford County, WI	$559
Dodge County, WI	$643
Door County, WI	$644
Dunn County, WI	$615
Eau Claire, WI	$647
Florence County, WI	$578
Fond du Lac, WI	$633
Forest County, WI	$558
Grant County, WI	$590
Green Bay, WI	$689
Green County, WI	$625
Green Lake County, WI	$551
Iowa County, WI	$623
Iron County, WI	$529
Jackson County, WI	$564
Janesville-Beloit, WI	$644
Jefferson County, WI	$675
Juneau County, WI	$587
Kenosha County, WI	$736
Lafayette County, WI	$562
Langlade County, WI	$530
Lincoln County, WI	$556
Madison, WI	$988
Manitowoc County, WI	$549
Marinette County, WI	$542
Marquette County, WI	$594
Menominee County, WI	$554
Milwaukee-Waukesha-West Allis, WI	$800
Monroe County, WI	$646
Oconto County, WI	$599
Oneida County, WI	$662
Oshkosh-Neenah, WI	$654
Pepin County, WI	$601
Polk County, WI	$628
Portage County, WI	$610
Price County, WI	$529
Racine, WI	$700
Richland County, WI	$575
Rusk County, WI	$552
Sauk County, WI	$671
Sawyer County, WI	$629

Shawano County, WI	$540
Sheboygan, WI	$640
Taylor County, WI	$551
Trempealeau County, WI	$564
Vernon County, WI	$584
Vilas County, WI	$557
Walworth County, WI	$707
Washburn County, WI	$585
Waupaca County, WI	$601
Wausau, WI	$653
Waushara County, WI	$533
Wood County, WI	$560

Wyoming

Area	Rent
Albany County, WY	$668
Big Horn County, WY	$565
Campbell County, WY	$801
Carbon County, WY	$689
Casper, WY	$746
Cheyenne, WY	$671
Converse County, WY	$673
Crook County, WY	$657
Fremont County, WY	$642
Goshen County, WY	$634
Hot Springs County, WY	$619
Johnson County, WY	$776
Lincoln County, WY	$683
Niobrara County, WY	$544
Park County, WY	$646
Platte County, WY	$562
Sheridan County, WY	$747
Sublette County, WY	$760
Sweetwater County, WY	$786
Teton County, WY	$1,149
Uinta County, WY	$597
Washakie County, WY	$611
Weston County, WY	$678

Source: U.S. Department of Housing and Urban Development
https://www.huduser.gov/portal/datasets/50per.html

Glossary

This glossary contains the most important terms used in this publication.

Cap   The maximum amount an insurance policy will cover for an item; for example, a cap on fine jewelry might by $1,500.

Claim   A report that you file with an insurance company if some or all of your personal property is damaged or destroyed.

Deductible   The amount of money you must pay out of pocket before an insurance policy kicks in.

Endorsement   Also called a trailer or a rider, an endorsement offers additional coverage for a category of items, such as electronics equipment.

Exclusion   Something not covered by insurance.

Floater   Offers additional coverage for a specific item, such as an antique firearm.

Peril   Something that causes harm or damage, such as a fire.

SOURCES

http://metcouncilonhousing.org/help_and_answers/if_you_want_to_break_your_lease

http://money.usnews.com/money/personal-finance/articles/2013/09/12/4-common-myths-about-renters-insurance

http://www.iii.org/article/your-renters-insurance-checklist

http://www.iii.org/sites/default/files/docs/pdf/III%20%20renters%209%202009final%20(2).pdf

http://www.investopedia.com/insurance/what-does-renters-insurance-cover/

http://www.moneycrashers.com/how-much-renters-insurance-need-cover/

http://www.netquote.com/home-insurance/renters-insurance-wont-cover

https://insurance.mo.gov/consumers/home/documents/RentersPolicyFP-7954.pdf

https://ohmyapt.apartmentratings.com/what-information-is-required-when-applying-for-renters-insurance.html

https://time.com/4217610/renting-first-apartment/

https://www.allstate.com/tools-and-resources/renters-insurance/what-does-renters-insurance-cover.aspx

https://www.apartmentguide.com/blog/things-to-think-about-before-renting/

https://www.esurance.com/insurance/renters/coverage

https://www.investopedia.com/articles/personal-finance/061515/4-things-landlords-are-not-allowed-do.asp

https://www.investopedia.com/articles/personal-finance/090315/millennials-guide-how-read-lease.asp

https://www.statefarm.com/insurance/home-and-property/renters/coverage-options

https://www.trustedchoice.com/renters-insurance/coverage-discounts/

https://www.trustedchoice.com/renters-insurance/coverage-faq/#1791072690

https://www.valuepenguin.com/homeowners-insurance-endorsements-scheduling

Weiss Ratings: What Our Ratings Mean

A   **Excellent.**   The company offers excellent financial security. It has maintained a conservative stance in its investment strategies, business operations and underwriting commitments. While the financial position of any company is subject to change, we believe that this company has the resources necessary to deal with severe economic conditions.

B   **Good.**   The company offers good financial security and has the resources to deal with a variety of adverse economic conditions. It comfortably exceeds the minimum levels for all of our rating criteria, and is likely to remain healthy for the near future. However, in the event of a severe recession or major financial crisis, we feel that this assessment should be reviewed to make sure that the firm is still maintaining adequate financial strength.

C   **Fair.**   The company offers fair financial security and is currently stable. But during an economic downturn or other financial pressures, we feel it may encounter difficulties in maintaining its financial stability.

D   **Weak.**   The company currently demonstrates what, in our opinion, we consider to be significant weaknesses which could negatively impact policyholders. In an unfavorable economic environment, these weaknesses could be magnified.

E   **Very Weak.**   The company currently demonstrates what we consider to be significant weaknesses and has also failed some of the basic tests that we use to identify fiscal stability. Therefore, even in a favorable economic environment, it is our opinion that policyholders could incur significant risks.

F   **Failed.**   The company is deemed failed if it is either 1) under supervision of an insurance regulatory authority; 2) in the process of rehabilitation; 3) in the process of liquidation; or 4) voluntarily dissolve after disciplinary or other regulatory action by an insurance regulatory authority.

+   The plus sign is an indication that the company is in the upper third of the letter grade.

-   The minus sign is an indication that the company is in the lower third of the letter grade.

U   Unrated. The company is unrated for one or more of the following reasons: (1) total assets are less than $1 million; (2) premium income for the current year was less than $100,000; or (3) the company functions almost exclusively as a holding company rather than as an underwriter; or, (4) in our opinion, we do not have enough information to reliably issue a rating.

Terms and Conditions

Weiss Ratings' Mission Statement
Weiss Ratings' mission is to empower consumers, professionals, and institutions with high quality advisory information for selecting or monitoring a financial services company or financial investment. In doing so, Weiss Ratings will adhere to the highest ethical standards by maintaining our independent, unbiased outlook and approach to advising our customers.

https://greyhouse.weissratings.com

Financial Ratings Series, published by Weiss Ratings and Grey House Publishing offers libraries, schools, universities and the business community a wide range of investing, banking, insurance and financial literacy tools. Visit www.greyhouse.com or https://greyhouse.weissratings.com for more information about the titles and online tools below.

- Weiss Ratings Financial Literacy Basics
- Weiss Ratings Financial Literacy: Planning For the Future
- Weiss Ratings Guide to Banks
- Weiss Ratings Guide to Credit Unions
- Weiss Ratings Guide to Health Insurers
- Weiss Ratings Guide to Property & Casualty Insurers
- Weiss Ratings Guide to Life & Annuity Insurers
- Weiss Ratings Investment Research Guide to Stocks
- Weiss Ratings Investment Research Guide to Bond & Money Market Mutual Funds
- Weiss Ratings Investment Research Guide to Stock Mutual Funds
- Weiss Ratings Investment Research Guide to Exchange-Traded Funds
- Weiss Ratings Consumer Guides
- Weiss Ratings Medicare Supplement Insurance Buyers Guide
- Financial Ratings Series Online – **https://greyhouse.weissratings.com**